The Skellig Story

The Skellig Story
ANCIENT MONASTIC OUTPOST

Des Lavelle

THE O'BRIEN PRESS
DUBLIN

First published 1976 by The O'Brien Press. Reprinted 1977, 1981.
First paperback edition 1987.
This updated edition first published 1993 by
The O'Brien Press Ltd.,
20 Victoria Road, Dublin 6, Ireland
Tel +353 1 4923333
Fax +353 1 4922777
e-mail books@obrien.ie
Web http://www.obrien.ie
Reprinted 1999

ISBN 0-86278-295-3

11 12 13 10 9 8 7 6
05 04 03 02 01 00 99

British Library Cataloguing-in-publication Data
A catalogue reference for this book is available from the British Library.

Maps: Adrian Slattery
Typesetting: The O'Brien Press Ltd.
Printing: Leinster Leader
Photographs: Des Lavelle

Contents

Foreword

The two Skellig islands are many times more important than either their size or location would suggest. In any world map of archaeology, the Skellig stands out in bold, conspicuous letters; similarly, in the ornithological world, the name of Skellig conveys a richness of seabird life which is not easily equalled.

And there is more: fascinating lighthouse history, magnificent cliff scenery, interesting local folklore, incredible richness in the surrounding ocean ... and there are many, many Skellig questions that do not have answers ...

But that is only part of the motivation for this book; the real reason is that these Skellig islands fascinate me. I have sailed around them, flown over them and dived on every sheer underwater cliff face beneath them; I have visited them to wander and wonder at least fifty times in 1990, and the same the year before, and the year before ... and by researching and writing and poring over a wide variety of photographs, I can be out there immediately in spirit, savouring, as George Bernard Shaw said about the place – 'the magic that takes you out, far out, of this time and this world'.

These spiritual visits are too wonderful to hide; I want to share them. But one must try to strike a balance of interest for the historian, the bird lover, the archaeology student, the day-visitor who needs to answer a multitude of queries and the Kerryman who hungers for more knowledge of his native ground.

Elsewhere in the book I have named the many individuals and services to whom I am indebted for their time, their interest and their assistance throughout the entire project, but I was fortunate to have one particularly steadfast and encouraging helper on my side from the outset – my all-enduring wife. For this reason, I dedicate the book: to Pat.

Des Lavelle, Valentia Island

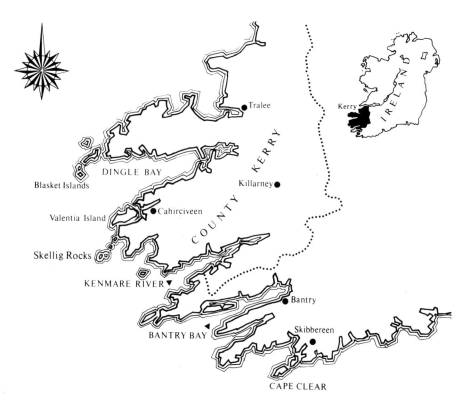

Tralee

Kerry

KERRY

DINGLE BAY

Blasket Islands

Killarney

Valentia Island ●Cahirciveen

COUNTY

Skellig Rocks

KENMARE RIVER▼

Bantry

BANTRY BAY ▲

Skibbereen

CAPE CLEAR

IRELAND

Kerry

Skellig Michael
LOCATION MAP

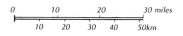

0   10   20   30 miles

10   20   30   40   50km

The Skellig Experience

The Skellig Experience Visitor Centre on Valentia Island is a major, weatherproof attraction which opened in 1992.

As well as being the launching point for a luxury 90-minute cruise around the Skellig islands, the Skellig Experience also 'transports' the Skellig islands across 8 miles (13km) of ocean. In a purpose-built interpretation centre on the waterfront of Valentia Island, the sights, sounds and stories of Skellig are readily accessible.

Four popular Skellig themes are illustrated and discussed by means of models, graphics, artifacts and an audio-visual presentation in an 80-seat theatre.

Included in the presentation are the life and times of the Early Christian monks in the island monasteries of the west coast of Ireland. A major feature of this section is a scaled-down replica of a monk's beehive hut from Skellig Michael.

The story of Skellig lighthouse – how it was built, its history, its lighthouse men and their involvement in many incidents from shipwreck to air-crash – is also covered. A reconstruction of a typical lighthouse operations room is featured in this section.

Life-size models of the seabirds of the coast and islands, together with information about their habitat and their oceanwide travels, are exhibited in a realistic cliff-face setting of native rock.

Finally, the underwater world of Skellig, with its rich and brilliantly coloured marine life, is displayed in colour photograph.

The centre's 15-minute audio-visual programme is a guided tour of ancient Skellig. It visits the old landing places, climbs the old stone stairways, tiptoes through the silent monastic village, and ascends the lonely hermit's cell at the island's pinnacle. En route it captures the many moods of Skellig – tranquillity, storm, isolation.

The interpretation of Skellig does not end as you leave the centre. The 90-minute cruise, which is an integral part of the Experience, provides a further on-the-spot informative commentary on all aspects of the islands, the coast and the ocean in between.

"Skellig Experience" Centre

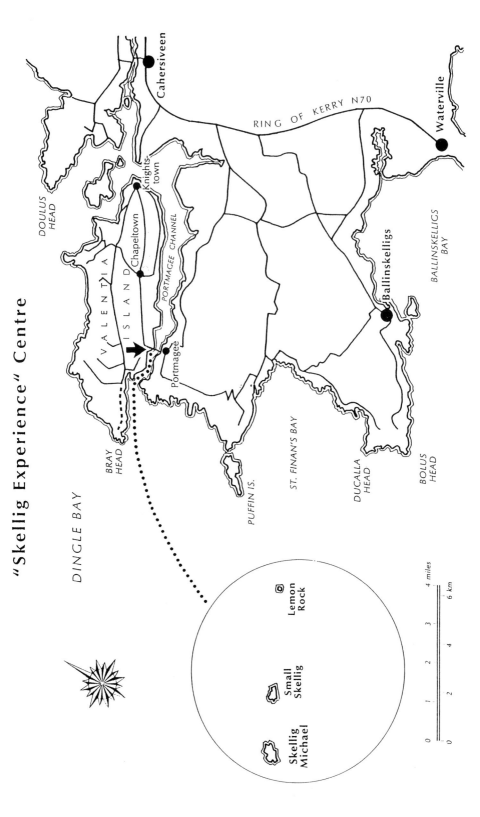

Acknowledgements

The author has been helped along over the years by many people, and would like to thank in particular the following: Miss M. O'Brien, Librarian, Cahirsiveen; Miss K. Turner, Kerry County Library; Mr. T. Armitage, Central Library; Mr. F.J. Ryan, Skerries; Mr. T. Shortt, Cahirsiveen; Mr. J. Shanahan, Portmagee; Mr. T. 'Busty' Burns, Valentia; Mr. P. O'Sullivan, C.B.S., Cahirsiveen; Mr. J. O'Reilly, Cork; Mr. A. Lidstrom, Umea, Sweden; Mr. P. Gallagher, Hon. Secretary, Valentia Lifeboat; Mr. Don Roberts, Kilkenny; The Secretary, Irish Wildbird Conservancy; Mr. P. Evans, Mr. O. Merne and Mr. A. Lack, for bird-counts and plant-lists; The Secretary, the Inspector and Marine Superintendent, and the Engineer in Chief, Irish Lights; The Principal and Assistant Keepers, Skellig Lighthouse; The Board of Trinity College Dublin; The Officers of the Royal Irish Academy, The Librarian, Bodleian Library, Oxford; The Archivist, Dept. of Irish Folklore, U.C.D., and the Directors of the National Museums of Dublin, Copenhagen and Oslo.

Photographic and darkroom facilities and much valuable advice on that subject were given by Padraig Kennelly, Tralee, and Robin Holder, Valentia Island.

ABOUT THE PHOTOGRAPHS
All the photographs – except where otherwise accredited – are by the author, shot over the years since 1972 – initially with a Pentax Spotmatic and three lenses, 28, 50, and 135mm, and later with a Nikon FG and two zoom lenses, 36-210mm.

The film used was whatever South Kerry's limited supplies offered – a sinful mixture of Kodax Tri X, Plus X, Kodachrome, Ektachrome, Fujichrome and Agfachrome – as well as Kodacolor negative which was coerced to yield black and white prints.

Early History and Legend

'Like two mighty ships, sailing along majestically with every shred of canvas set'; such are the Skellig Rocks – Skellig Michael and Small Skellig – seven sea miles off Valentia on the Atlantic coast of Kerry. These great towering sea-crags, steeped as they are in history and legend, become daily more and more important in this particular age of bustle, pollution and all-consuming 'progress'. The archaeology of Skellig, the bird life, the seals, the wide-open, timeless scenery – for one reason or another there is a balm for every soul on the Skelligs.

A shipwreck of some 1400 B.C., brought about by the magic of the Tuatha de Danann, is our first reference to Skellig, when Milesius, leader of the early invasions of Ireland, lost two sons in the area.

Irr lost his life upon the western main;
Skellig's high cliffs the hero's bones contain.
In the same wreck Arranan too was lost,
Nor did his corpse e'er touch Ierne's coast.

Another legendary visitor of some importance about the year A.D. 200 was Daire Domhain – King of the World. He rested a while at the Skellig before his attack on the nearby coast and his battle of a year-and-a-day with Fionn Mac Cool's Fianna at Ventry.

In the 5th century, Duagh, King of Munster, fled for his life to the isolation of the Skellig when pursued by Aengus, King of Cashel, and another legend tells that St. Malachy, when driven from his monastery in Bangor, also fled to Skellig for refuge.

And what a real place of refuge this is! Landing on the smaller Skellig is generally impossible, and the larger, twin-pinnacled Skellig Michael – even granted that a landing may be possible – calls for a stout heart and a steady head to master the island's steep faces of shaley sandstone which reach 217m in height.

Little wonder that this island, like other similar high places, became dedicated to Michael, Archangel, taking on the name by which it is known today, 'Sceilig Mhichíl'.

It was here, says the legend, on this 'certain crag surrounded on

Annals of Innisfallen. Bodleian Library. ms. Rawl. B.503. f.14 r. mid column 3, in Irish. 'Skellig was plundered by the heathen and Etgal was carried off and he died of hunger on their hands.'

every side by the eddies of the great sea ... distant a day's sail from the land', that St. Michael appeared together with others of the Heavenly Host to help St. Patrick banish the serpents and other evil things of Ireland into the sea. And with relatively early Christianity came the founding of a monastery on the rock – a small enclosure of stone huts and oratories which, though long since unoccupied, still stands to this day near the island's northern pinnacle, some 182m above the sea.

And, as if this outpost was not tranquil enough for the hardy monks, an associated hermit's retreat on the island's 217m southern pinnacle was the ultimate refinement of isolation! The founder of this monastery is not named. Current tradition – without any supporting evidence – attributes it to one of two St. Fionáns, and the influence of 'Fionán' is certainly strong in local placenames, but another, seldom-mentioned, possible founder member of the monastic community is St. Suibhne of Skellig, who is listed under April 28th in the Martyrology of Tallaght which was written at the end of the 8th century. Nor is the exact date of the foundation known, but the style of building suggests the 6th century onwards. There are other examples of this style and this date at many points of Ireland's west coast – but none in such perfect repair as the Skellig Michael monastery.

In A.D. 795, the first Viking attacks from Scandinavia were launched on the Irish coast, and the Skellig settlement did not escape for long. The early Irish manuscripts, the *Annals of Innisfallen, Annals of Ulster* and *Annals of the Four Masters*, contain only scant information on these raids, and there are no written sources in Scandinavia from the Viking period, but we do know these sleek, clinker-built longships, with their high graceful bow and shallow draught were of advanced design in their age; some of them had a crew of 40, but others were big vessels of up to 40m which could be rowed or sailed at 10 knots and could carry several hundred men.

In A.D. 812, the Skellig monastery was sacked. Again in 823, as reported in the *Annals of Ulster* and *Annals of Innisfallen*, the Vikings came and this time they took Etgal, Abbot of Skellig, and starved him to death. The years 833 and 839 saw further attacks when Turgesius, Sovereign of the Danes, swept through the area.

John Henry Newman, in his *Historical Sketches*, gives a grim description of the Viking's technique:

> the sea, instead of being a barrier, was the very element and condition of his victories and it carried him upon its bosom, up and down, with an ease and expedition which even in open country was impracticable. They ravaged far and wide at will, and no retaliation on them was possible, for these pirates, unlike their more civilised brethren of Algiers or Greece, had not a yard of territory, a town, or a fort, no property but their vessels, no subjects but their

Annals of the Four Masters. R.I.A. C3. 422v., in Irish.
Line 1 A.D. 1044.
Line 5 Aodh of Skellig Michael died.

crews. They were not allowed either to inherit or transmit the booty which these piratical expeditions collected ... 'Never to sleep under a smoke-burnished roof, never to fill the cup over a cheerful hearth' was their boast and principle. If they drank, it was not for good company but by degrading extravagance, to rival the beasts of prey and blood in their wild brutality.

Patrick Foley in his book, *The Ancient and Present State of the Skelligs, Blasket Islands, etc,* adds:

They ran into land and set fire to villages and massacred the inhabitants. Whilst so engaged, their favourite sport was the tossing of infants on top of their lances to and from each other ... Laws, religion and society they had no regard for. Both on sea and land their hands were always

14

steeped in blood, murder and plunder. It was only when these pirates plundered and murdered each other that they finally collapsed.

But in spite of the attacks and the plundering, the monastic community on Skellig survived. In A.D. 860 some rebuilding was done and detailed studies of the now-ruined hermitage on the Southern Peak suggest that this too may have been a 9th century construction. In the year 885 Flan MacCallach, Abbot of Skellig, died. In 950 the *Annals of the Four Masters* has the brief entry that Blathmac of Skellig passed away. Legend tells that in 993 Viking Olav Trygvasson, who was later to become King of Norway and whose son Olav II, was to become patron saint of Norway, was baptised by a Skellig hermit. The final report in this era, from the *Annals of the Four Masters*, dated 1044, says simply: 'Aodh of Skellig died.' This is all the information we have from that period.

How these ascetic monks ever contrived to live on this 18 hectare crag is a mystery by today's standards. In summer, no doubt, they enjoyed seabirds, eggs and fish, but winter must have brought months of lean isolation. The small hide-covered boats of the period were hardly adequate for a regular supply ferry, and it seems unlikely that they lived as well as the contemporary settlers of Church Island, Valentia, who enjoyed oats, barley, wheat, rye, cod, wrasse, gannet, shag, goose, duck, cormorant, seal, goat, pig, sheep, ox and pony!

Sadly, few artifacts have ever come to light to give us any insight into the occupations of the Skellig monastic community. During the early lighthouse work in the 19th century two items were reported: 'Here we saw a small bronze figure of our Saviour, about four inches [101mm] in height, found by the workmen in excavating. It was impossible to conceive anything more barbarous than this image, or nearer in resemblance to the rudest idol.' Another version says: 'A rude bronze crucifix with crown and kilted tunic, about four inches high [101mm], was found among the huts by the lighthouse work-men.' Fortunately, this item finally found its way to the National Museum, but the second piece, 'A clay figure of the Virgin', is no longer extant.

A stone 'water-font', some 197 x 114 x 127mm, which had been in the large oratory of Skellig monastery as far back as living memory

A stone water-font from Skellig thought to date from the 17th century. It had always been in the large oratory of the monastery, but is currently retained by the Office of Public Works.

can recall, is currently retained by the Office of Public Works. It is thought to be late 17th or 18th century, and its presence on Skellig may be related to the medieval pilgrimage era.

It is pleasant to dream that Skellig manuscripts similar to the Book of Kells or the other Irish annals might exist and one day be discovered, but the harsh realities of the island must favour other conclusions: with minimal domestic equipment and few, if any, personal possessions other than the smock and cloak which they wore, membership of the Skellig monastery must have been a hard exercise in mere survival alone.

Welsh cleric and historian, Giraldus Cambrensis, reported at the end of the 12th century that the Skellig community moved base to Ballinskelligs 'on the continent', but the island monastery did remain occupied and in repair, and it is a fact that one particular church building in the monastic enclosure was extended in those middle ages. The ecclesiastical taxation of A.D. 1300 refers to the 'Church of St. Michael's Rock' having a valuation of 20s. (£1).

Opposite: There are no written reports in Scandinavia from the Viking period, but excavated renovated artifacts, like this 'Oseberg' Viking ship, speak eloquently for the ship-building skills of that era.

Pilgrimage

Occupied or otherwise, Skellig Michael featured as a place of pilgrimage and penance for many years. Early in the 16th century the Register of Primate Dowdall of Armagh lists Skellig Michael as one of the principal penitential stations for the performance of public penance, and there is a record too of one sinner who was obliged to make a visit to the Skellig and other penitential stations as penance for murdering his own son.

Two centuries later, writers such as Friar O'Sullivan were still referring to Skellig Michael, and to pilgrims coming from all over Ireland and Europe at Eastertime – not so much to visit the monastery, it would appear, but to perform the nerve-racking, difficult climb to follow the Stations of the Cross and finally kiss a standing stone slab overhanging the sea near the isolated hermitage of the Needle's Eye, on the 217m southern pinnacle of the island.

Early writers report the climax of this climb in great detail, describing the pilgrim inching his way outwards astride a narrow projecting spit of rock, reciting certain prayers and finally kissing the carving at the extremity before retiring to safety.

Fortunately not many visitors today are brave enough or imprudent enough to risk their lives in undertaking this hazardous adventure. Nor is there any stone slab to kiss now; it disappeared about 1977! It was not stolen, nor was it pushed over. More likely the wind and rain of a thousand years took their toll. And although amateur divers searched the depths of Blue Cove directly below, no trace was ever found. Perhaps this piece of Skellig history was shattered into fragments in its 217m tumble.

'There is still living a gentleman', wrote Lady Chatterton in *Rambles in the South of Ireland*, 1839, 'who *walked* out to the eternity of this spit, and performing a regular pirouette, *returned!* However, the guides always encouraged the pilgrims by assuring them that no one was ever lost but an Englishman, who undertook the pilgrimage in order to ridicule the custom, and falling from the spit was drowned.

The cartographer of 1567 confuses the Blasket Sound and the Dursey Sound, but nonetheless the two Skellig islands can be recognised (marked with arrow at top of map).

From this circumstance a saying, much in use in this country, as applied to persons of ridiculously inordinate desires, has its origins. It runs thus: "More water," *arsa an Sasanach agus é á bhádhaidh*, or "More water," says the Englishman and he drowning. The tradition being that the unfortunate Sasanach found himself so long falling, as to call out for the rising of the sea in order to put an end to his tumble.'

19

Charles Smith, in his *Ancient and Present State of the County of Kerry*, 1756, shows a reproduction of 'The Skellig from the South West', but its gross inaccuracy proves clearly that the artist was never near the rock. His description of the monastery wells being 'a few yards above sea level', when in fact they are at a height of some 182m, leads to a similar conclusion. On the other hand, the general difficulty of the climb to the Needle's Eye is very real, and due to looseness caused by the burrowings of a plague of rabbits, it is probably more hazardous now than ever before.

In August 1779, one famous seaman, who certainly was no repentant pilgrim, almost came to grief upon the Skellig. The French Archives contain details from the Admiral's own pen: 'At 8.00p.m. Mizen Head lay astern, and with a fine breeze the squadron stood N.N.W. along the ironbound coast of Kerry. By noon we were five miles S.S.W. of Great Skellig.'

Here the fleet ran into a calm, and after some time the Admiral's flagship began to drift dangerously close to the Skellig – so close that her largest rowing boat had to be lowered to tow her clear. But the tale does not end there. The oarsmen were all Irishmen who had

A View of the Great SCELIG ISLAND from the South West

The erroneous impression of Skellig Michael from Smith's The Ancient and Present State of the County of Kerry.

been 'pressed into service' against their wishes, and as soon as the flagship was out of danger – but still becalmed – they cut the tow rope and headed for Valentia at their best speed.

The flagship they had abandoned at the Skellig was the 42-gun *Bonhomme Richard* and the Admiral they had outwitted was that master privateer, John Paul Jones.

Early in the 19th century, on the annual Feast of St. Michael, the parish priest of Ballinskelligs, Fr. Diarmuid O'Sullivan, used to visit Skellig Michael by boat to offer Mass on the island. Many people would travel with the priest on this pilgrimage, and the details of one particular visit which was marred by a sudden gale have been handed down in verse by the Iveragh poet, Tomás Ruadh Ua Suilliobháin – 1785-1848.

Maidean Bhog, Áluinn, I mBáidh Na Scealg

Maidean bhog, áluinn, i mBáidh na Scealg,
Dul ag triall chum Aifrinn ghrádhmhair Dé,
D'éirigh an tsuail ró-mhór 'san bhfarraige,
Le fuadar fearthaine, d'arduigh gaoth.
Do mhachtnuigh an chriú, 'gus is umhal do chasadar,
Ag deanamh an chuain anuas chum Dairbhre,
'Nuair bhéic an fear stiúir, as mo shuan do phreabas-sa;
Do bhíos im' chodladh is dúisigheadh mé.

Cia chífeadh an bád ar bháidh an mhaidean úd,
Sáth' sé maide uirthe, is do b'árd í a léim,
'Nuair scaoileadar cnáib agus gárdaidhe rámha uirthe
Gach clár ag cnagadh, agus í ag rás mar philéar!
Do dheineamar í stiúradh ar chúrsa tarraingthe,
Sruthanna ag brúghadh le siubhal na hanairte,
Ní raibh luascadh ar an lín ó'n mBaoi go Daingean siar,
Go ndeachamair go Carraig ghlas árd na Naomh.

Bhí Carraig Lomáin mar chráin ag screadadh rómhainn,
Ar tí sinn d'alpadh, le n-ár dtaoibh chlé;
Bealach na n-éigh do ghéim mar tharbh romhainn,
Is dar ndóigh níor thaise do'n Ghearánaigh éigheamh
Céad moladh le hÍosa Críost nár cailleadh sinn!
Is ná fuairtheas sinn sínte i nduibheagán farraige,

Acht fanam' arís go dtigidh an chalma,
Agus racham dho'n charraig le congnamh Dé.

Do bhí an tAthair Diarmuid go dian ag agairt
Ar Rígh na nAingeal an chriú theacht saor,
Agus do chualathas shuas é i n-uachtar Pharathais.
'Nuair adubhairt an phaidir ós ár gcionn go léir.
Do ghlanamair poinnte Rinn' gil' Cathrach,
Bhí an Góilín shíos go mín, tais, calma,
Níor stadamair de'n scríb go ndeachamair dho'n Chalath.
Is d'ólamair fleagan 'dtig Sheain Mhic Aodha.

Bhí an fhuireann úd fuar tar éis uamhain na fairrge,
'Nuair do b'fhonn leis an sagart an chriú do théadh
Do thóg sé leis suas iad go cuan an mhaitheasa,
Ar bhruach an teaghlaigh úd Sheain Mhic Aodha.
D'fhanamair annsúd ag diúgadh an bharaille,
Mar a raibh fairsing de'n lionn le fonn d'a scaipeadh againn;
Sinn ag faire ar gach uain go h-uair na maidne,
Agus an uamhain gur sheasaimh go fáinne an lae.

Is deacair an bád do cháineadh, geallaim díbh,
Le grásta an Athair-Mhic tháinig saor,
Thug an fhuireann úd slán ó Bháidh na Scealg
An lá bhí anfadh árd 'san aer.
Ca bhfuil an t-árthach le fagh" do b'fhearra,
Do ghearrfadh casán tré lár na mara?
Dá dheascaibh sin táim-se fágaint barra
Ag an mbáidín greannta sin Sheain Uí Néill!

Translation (Des Lavelle)

A morning sea by glass,
In Skelligs Bay,
Upon our way
To serve God's loving mass.
A rise of swell,
And rain as well,
And storm soon came to pass.

Our prudent crewmen frowned,
But not for long.

22

Unwise to carry on,
And to Valentia Sound
We turned our yawl.
The helmsman's call
Enlivened all around.

Since early dawn arrived,
Our oar-blades light,
Our oarlocks tight,
Set every plank alive.
While bullet-speed she sped,
No ripple spread
By Beara, Dingle or the Skelligside.

That roaring Lemon stone,
That hungry sow,
Would take us now.
The Puffin's Strait of Groans,
Gearánaigh gap,
A baited trap,
Bull-bellowing with foam.

To Jesus praises be.
We were not lost,
Nor paid the cost
Beneath the deepest sea.
So we shall 'tend
The tempest's end
Where e'er the haven be.

Dear Father Diarmuid prayed
To bring us through.
The angels too
Our words to God relayed.
Reen point we passed,
And safe at last,
To Seán Mac Aodha's we strayed.

To drink a warming brew,
A flagon glass,
The night to pass,
A porter barrel too
to be consumed,
To lick our wounds
Until the day broke through.

Neill's boat was not to blame –
Nor oars nor men.
'Tis prudent when
The pathways through the main
Turn dark and white,
Turn back; take flight;
And live to fight again.

Another tale of an eventful Skellig visit is the story of Ana Ní Áine
– the old woman of Kenmare. Freely translated from Robin Jackson's
Scéalta ón mBlascaod, it runs like this:

When I was a young woman my father had a
pleasure boat and many strangers would come to
our house to sail from place to place with him. One
fine Autumn day myself and another girl decided to
accompany them to the Skellig; there was also a
young priest in the boat with us.

We set out for Skellig but before we reached the
island a dreadful darkness approached from the West.
My father wanted to put the boat about and head
for home, but the others would not hear of this.

The dark cloud steadily approached with great gusts
of wind. The priest looked towards it. 'There is some
mystery in that cloud,' he said.

It was now bearing down on us until it was almost
upon the boat, and then we could see that within
the cloud was the spirit of a woman!

The priest jumped to his feet, put his confessional
stole around his neck and took his book in his hands.
He spoke to the woman and asked her what caused
her unrest.
'I killed a person,' said the woman.
'That's not what damned you,' said the priest.
'I killed two people,' said the woman.
'It's not that either,' said the priest.
'I killed my own unbaptised child – whose father
was a priest,' said the woman.
'That indeed is the cause of your damnation,' said
the priest.

'The sense of solitude, the vast heaven above and the sublime monotonous motion of the sea beneath ...'
Part of the monastery with Small Skellig behind.

Then he began to read from his book and in a short moment the released spirit rose in a great flash and disappeared from sight.

The storyteller concludes: 'We didn't continue to the Skellig that day; we returned home.'

Surprisingly, one cannot find many such tales of the supernatural in relation to Skellig. Maxwell's *A Book of Islands* leaves one such situation hanging in mid-air:

Everything was so peaceful that I climbed down to a concealed lighthouse on the island's outer flank to see if the night could be spent there. Meanwhile Tom pursued his archaeological study of the ruins.

The lighthouse men gave no encouragement. Nobody, they said, was allowed to stay without permission from Trinity House in Dublin. Nor would anybody in his senses want to stay there. The island was haunted and things often thumped on their own bolted door at night while the banshees wailed from the graveyard.

Surely, I suggested, this would be the shearwaters, but they replied with scorn that they knew all the birds as they had nothing else to study. It could be the monks with uneasy consciences, or it could be the poor souls whose lives they had been unable to save after a shipwreck a few years ago – or it could be something else.

Tom was sitting on the ground looking pale and shaken when I returned. Before I could speak he said: 'For God's sake let's get off this island at once.' And then he added: 'Something nearly pushed me over the cliff when I was climbing to some nettles just below the oratory, and after I had got back to Christ's Saddle some force struck which threw me flat on my face.'

Coming from so powerful and fearless a man as Tom this was extraordinary and, on top of what the lighthouse men had been saying, extremely sinister. Our descent to the boat was made with backward glances ...

Over the years the penitential nature of the early Skellig pilgrimages developed into something quite different. Patrick Foley puts it this way: 'Generally, in the latter days of these pilgrimages, the religious ceremonies were attended almost exclusively by girls and bachelors who were considered duly eligible for marriage. Of course, the idea was to spend Holy Week in fasting and praying. However, it transpired that many of the young "eligibles" instead of fasting and praying, visited the island with the intention of courting, dancing, drinking and enjoying themselves in other various amusements ...'

Finally, not only were the annual pilgrimages denounced from the altar, but when the practice persisted the police got orders to clear the rock.

Possibly from these pilgrimages, possibly from the changes of the Gregorian calendar in 1782, or possibly because the abbot of the early monastery outranked the local bishop, a peculiar custom evolved –

Opposite: The final flight of steps from Christ's Saddle to the monastery plateau.

a tradition that the annual ecclesiastical period of Lent arrived later
to Skellig than it did to the mainland, and consequently that marriage
could be contracted on the Skellig at times when this would be
impossible on the mainland of Ireland. it is not known if anyone ever
availed of this facility, but the Skelligs Lists – the annual, anonymous
and highly defamatory poems of the era – suggested many possibilities:

> And down in the cabin,
> As Skellig draws near,
> See Maggie so strongly caressed.
> And Patsy McCann whispers
> 'Shortly, my dear,
> We'll hold our heads high like the rest!'
> The Hegarty lad
> From the Strand Street bohaun,
> Is there with his Mary tonight.
> The Abbot of Skellig
> Will wed them at dawn –
> A wedding that cannot be white…

Of the many Skellig Lists retained in the Archives of the Department
of Irish Folklore, U.C.D., the List of 1922 from Lispole, in the Dingle
peninsula is unique insofar as it deals – in humorous fashion – more
with the nautical difficulties of sailing to Skellig than with the
characteristics of the couples involved.

This Skellig group is depicted as departing from Minard harbour,
but there was only one small boat – and that was already full …

> Then up stepped Thomas Moran when he saw his
>   craft was gone,
> Saying comrades dear and maidens fair, I have for
>   you a plan.
> If you'll agree and follow me, we'll sail for Skellig
>   too
> In a ship that's far more stately than a little mean
>   canoe.
> That barque lies over yonder we'll set afloat again,
> And pack the holes up safely with bags of barley
>   grain.

You need not be the least afraid; believe me when
    I say
She'll float as safe as Noah's Ark with you across the
    main.
Away we went with one consent to where *Ruthickman*
    lay,
And soon we had her floating on the waters of the
    bay.
The passengers, they went on deck, and all prepared
    to go.
'Twas then they found they had no sails,
Which filled their hearts with woe.
'Don't worry boys,' said Moran, 'the ladies' shawls
    will do.'
He asked them and he got them – without a grumble
    too.
They tied them up along the masts, and when they
    caught the wind,
'Twas quick and soon they sailed away, and left
    Minard behind.

Skellig Lists such as these, some of them containing up to forty verses – humorous, satirical, vicious – were common throughout Munster from Dingle to Cork for at least the past 140 years, but perhaps it is just as well that the custom has died out recently, or libel actions would be widespread.

This letter, received by a Cork printer in 1834, must be typical of the irate feelings of Skelligs List victims.

> Sir, You are requested to take notice that I will hold you responsible for any liberties taken with the names of Mary Ellen Harris, Sarah Harris and Eliza Driscoll, they being members of my family, and having received intelligence of some person or persons wishing to expose them in the Skelligs Lists which are to come to and through your press, I am determined to indict all persons concerned if there is anything prejudicial to their person, interest or character in any manner.
>
> *Hugh Driscoll,*
> *January 28, 1834.*

The Sea Journey

The modern Skellig 'pilgrim' might well assume that all the ancient problems of access to the island have been eliminated in this age of sturdy, sea-worthy, diesel-engined boats; but he would be wrong! True, the modern local boat is far removed from the hide-covered craft of old, and true, it would be quite possible nowadays to beat a reasonable passage to Skellig through most weather – fog, calm or Force 6 – but irrespective of the mode, comfort or difficulty of the sea journey from the mainland, it is the sea conditions immediately around the small, exposed landing of Skellig Michael which dictate access to the island.

Of course it is never necessary to travel all the way to Skellig to assess the landing conditions; all the local, mainland boatmen have a yardstick closer to home which will give them a very accurate appraisal of the possibilities. A Valentia man, for instance, can look at the Holy Ground rocks – 25.7km from Skellig – and decide on that observation if a landing is feasible. A Derrynane man may take one look at The Pigs outside his own harbour and base his decision on the conditions there. This is something that frequently baffles the visitor. On what appears to be a perfect summer's day, no boatman will take a Skellig party to sea!

So you must sit and wait for tomorrow. And ponder that this inaccessibility – in an age when we have access to the moon, is all part of the powerful magnetism of Skellig, the enhanced attraction of the unattainable!

In winter it is out of the question. Even a whole week without wind in the period November to March – an unlikely occurrence at best – would hardly be sufficient to calm the ocean around Skellig. During this season, Skellig cliffs are sea-lashed from every side. Great long swells, which may have travelled 2000 miles from some distant depression, mingle with local gales to create a terrible fury in which Skellig landing is scarcely visible. Winter wave crests will break 10m high over the pier and reach 45m up along the lighthouse road, as

On the horizon 8.5 miles (14km) south-west of Valentia Island, Small Skellig (left) and Skellig Michael (right).
(PHOTO: P. KENNELLY, TRALEE)

evidenced again in February 1988 when some modern Office of Public Works' work-buildings – together with sections of the roadway on which they stood – were hurled around and wrecked by storm waves. The receding turmoil of such wave-troughs will expose ragged seaweed stumps, sponges and anemones on the rock faces which are normally 10m below the mean surface! And this is the sheltered side of the island!

From April onwards, conditions can be expected to improve, and on fine summer days boats from Valentia, Portmagee, Ballinskelligs and Derrynane frequently provide a service for visitors to Skellig.

The traveller of 100 years ago could hire a rowing boat and four oarsmen exclusively for a Skellig trip for 25s. (£1.25) a day. Such an outing – a full, tiring day in any sense – was not for everyone, and even as late as the 1960s a Skellig trip was still quite a rarity. By 1970, tourism demand prompted one fishing boat or two to 'double up' as Skellig passenger boats on a more frequent basis; in 1973 the visitor had a choice of five boats – at a fare of £3 per person. And by 1990, the team of monastery guides employed by the Office of Public Works were hard pressed to cater for the large numbers of visitors, as ten boats from four harbours ran a busy Skellig service at £15 per person! But the elements were still master, giving the open-boat passenger a sunburn or a soaking, a wonderful experience or a bad fright, all at the whim of the wind. And it was also in 1990 that a new concept was born: to offer the Skellig enthusiast the option of circumnavigating the islands in a purpose-built, covered, passenger ship and of enjoying the Skellig story through the medium of the mainland-based Skellig Experience Visitor Centre on Valentia Island.

But for the moment, let's experience a Skellig trip from the hazy days of 1975.

It is 10.45a.m. on a fine summer's morning at Knightstown harbour, Valentia Island. The Shannon/Fastnet weather forecast – 'South-west 2/3; Visibility 25 miles (41km); 1033 millibars; Steady' indicates a good day for Skellig, and one of the local boats is preparing to make the trip. Half-a-dozen passengers step on board, with lunch boxes well packed for a full day's outing, and a selection of sweaters and rain coats – 'just in case'! They are foreign tourists and this is typical. Relatively few local Irish people visit Skellig, while foreigners of many nations can speak with authority and enthusiasm on all our national monuments and natural history.

'Cast off!' We have a brief stop at nearby Renard Point pier to pick up two more passengers and then we set off southwards through the five-mile corridor of Valentia harbour. On either hand, pebble beaches slope up to green field, yellow bog and blue mountain as we head for Portmagee, our final pick-up point before the open sea.

Kindred spirits on board recognise one another instantly across barriers of language, race and age in the spontaneous camaraderie of a shared shipboard adventure. Binoculars are compared with interest and the merits of German, Japanese and Russian brand-names are extolled. At least there is consensus on one point: 7 x 50 is the most suitable for boat-work where motion must be considered. Cameras, similarly, are much in evidence from the Hasselblad to the

A winter storm roars around Skellig, sending spray hurtling to the lighthouse – and higher.

Box Brownie. They may vary in quality and operation but the end products are very similar: memories of a certain summer's day.

Some diving black guillemots (*Cepphus grylle*), red-legged, black-beaked, and really as much white as black in appearance, occupy our attention. They spend their lives – summer and winter – here in the sheltered shallows of the bay and seldom venture out to the open sea. Yet, of all the seabirds, their nests are the most difficult to find.

One-legged at the water's edge on Reen-a-Rea Point stands a forlorn heron (*Ardea cinerea*), grey and sombre. Hump-backed, he waits for low water to go fishing. The wash from our passing boat slops about his knees, but it doesn't bother him.

Valentia bridge and Portmagee village are reached, and soon left behind. Our channel widens and Valentia's Bray Head, one of the Western extremities of the Irish coast, towers high on our right hand. On the left, we round Horse Island, local home of the lesser black-back gull (*Larus fuscus*), and at last we catch our first glimpse of Skellig, directly ahead and 7 miles (11km) away. This is the transition point between harbour and ocean and we feel the first gentle touch of the Atlantic in one of her kinder moods. Our course is 225º (C.), speed 7½ knots; destination: 51º 46' 20" N. 10º 32' 58" W., E.T.A. 12.55p.m., local time!

One of the younger passengers wonders if he may steer the boat for a while? And indeed he may. In these fine conditions the skipper is only too happy to hand over the wheel temporarily and take the opportunity to chat with the other passengers.

The vast panorama of the open sea expands around us as we forge ahead: the Blasket islands, 15 miles (27km) away to the north, a wide, empty horizon to the west, the two Skelligs and the Lemon Rock to the south-west, Puffin Island, rich bird-sanctuary of the Irish Wildbird Conservancy, and more miles of endless ocean to the south, and astern of us, the old red sandstone fingertips of Kerry's Macgillycuddy Reeks digging their nails into the sea. Out here, we meet the oceanic seabirds, guillemots, puffins, razorbills… swimming, flying, diving and making their living in various ways. An alarmed puffin surfaces too near the boat and amuses everyone by trying to take off in a panic and making a fiasco of it! He changes his mind and dives again to safety. To the west, flocks of noisy kittiwakes are vigorously working a shoal of sprats, and farther on, the black, triangular dorsal fin of a basking shark (*Cetorhinus maximus*), protrudes 1m above the surface of the sea. This remarkable giant – which may be as long as our boat – wanders slowly about the tide-streams, his awesome, gaping white mouth doing nothing more sinister than collecting microscopic plankton! If we take the boat too near, he simply slides down out of sight for a few moments and returns to his meal of surface plankton when all is clear. But sometimes we can quietly place a diver-photographer in the water in the shark's path, in search of an exciting

Skellig Michael

portrait as the monster passes by...

The first gannet – a reconnaissance outrider from Small Skellig – flies overhead on a ceremonial circuit of inspection. He is followed by others and still more, and as we approach the island a thousand gannets are in the air around us. Another thousand – it would appear

– occupy every visible ledge on Small Skellig, and as many more are plummeting like guided missiles into a fish shoal on the Northern side of the island. Where could you better this incredible experience? Possibly one place in the world! Only St. Kilda in the Outer Hebrides can boast more gannets than Small Skellig's 23,000 pairs. *'Regardez le phoque!' 'Kijk naar de zeehonden!' 'Féach an rón glas!''Seals! Seals! There on the rocks!'* Pointing fingers are outstretched and there is a jumble of excited languages and the cameras are re-trained and re-focussed and re-shot – and ultimately re-loaded with feverish haste.

Eventually Skellig Michael, our final goal, looms high above us, solid, massive, awe-inspiring, its sheer cliffs leading all the way to heaven. We throttle back and slip in alongside the tiny pier where one of the lighthouse men is waiting to lend a hand. Our lines are made fast. The engine is stopped. It is 12.55p.m., a modern pilgrimage to Skellig has begun – and nobody will dream of leaving this magical place until the evening is well advanced!

Up to the Monastery

The lands of the mainland monastery at Ballinskelligs were disposed of in the 16th century, and included in the lease to Gyles Clinsher in 1578 was 'a small island called Skellig Michell...' Later, the island, which certainly was uninhabited by that time, passed to John Butler of Waterville for rental of 'two hawks and a quantity of puffin feathers yearly'. In fact, the 'quantity' of feathers amounted to some 18 stone (114kg) which represented an enormous number of puffins. About 1820, the body which is now the Commissioners of Irish Lights bought the island for the purpose of erecting a lighthouse. In 1871, shortly before the Office of Public Works took over responsibility for the maintenance of the monastic site, Lord Dunraven produced the first detailed archaeological account of Skellig Michael, describing the whole monastic establishment rather as it still is today – a main enclosure of old stone dwellings and oratories, with some associated outbuildings, terraces and pathways throughout the island. Certain renovations to the monastic site have been attributed to 'the light-house workmen who ... in 1838, built some objectionable modern walls'. Another report of 1892 says: 'We cannot conclude this account without protesting strongly against the way in which repairs are being carried on at Skellig Michael by the Board of Works.

'At the time of the visit of the Cambrian and Irish archaeologists an ordinary mason was seen calmly tinkering away at the ruins, pulling down a bit here and building up a bit there in imitation of the old style of work, without any kind of superintendence whatever. The vandalism perpetrated some time ago by the same authorities, at Inishmurray, is being repeated here with a vengeance.'

Were these outbursts justified or was the wording a little too strong? I think these words of 1892 were right. And indeed, environmental watchdogs were again growling – and perhaps not in vain – about some aspects of the repair, reconstructions and weedkiller-usage of

Previous page: Cell E, Skellig Michael. The stairway in the left foreground has been removed and re-routed to the right as part of the modern renovation work.

The entrance to the monastery enclosure.
(PHOTO: OFFICE OF PUBLIC WORKS)

the 1980s. In any event, for one's enjoyment today, it is better to see Skellig not in the light of 19th or 20th century maintenance, but in the deeper context of the Early Christian design, labour and accom-

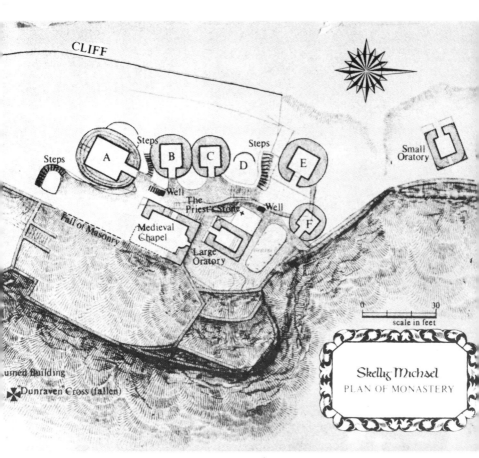

CLIFF

Steps

Steps

A   B   C   D   E

Well

The Priest's Stone

Well

F

Steps

Fall of Masonry

Medieval Chapel

Large Oratory

Small Oratory

0   30
scale in feet

ruined Building

Dunraven Cross (fallen)

Skellig Michael
PLAN OF MONASTERY

This plan is based on the plan from Lord Dunraven's Notes on Irish Architecture *but the author has added additional detail and used a different code for the dwellings. In the 1980s conspicuous alterations included: the removal of the steps between A and B, and the erection of a wall there; the re-routing of the steps between D and E; the clearing and reconstruction of the terrace levels in front of A, B, C, D, E; the reconstruction of the small oratory.*

plishment of this initial enormous feat. There are three ancient access paths cut and built into the rock faces from sea level up to the monastery, 182m above: the direct and steep eastern climb from Blind Man's Cove, the southern, part modern, zigzag path from Cross Cove, and the steep northern path from Blue Cove which joins the southern route at Christ's Saddle, 120m above the sea.

The eastern climb leads very steeply up the sheer face immediately above the landing. Parts of it have fallen away and become overgrown, but the principal reason why it is not used, or even seen today, is because the lighthouse road-builders of 1820 blew away all the lower approaches to this route. This inaccessibility is a blessing in disguise, as most of the remaining sections of the path are hazardous in the extreme. But what a beautiful route this is, with much more interesting stonework than the other climbs. Near the top of this path, before it reaches the monastery enclosure, is the island's third well which has not been mentioned by any of the early chroniclers. Here also, re-

Engraving from Lord Dunraven's Notes on Irish Architecture, *1875, this gives a rather elaborate and misleading impression of the site. This beautiful cross had fallen, broken in two and become completely overgrown until its rediscovery in 1974.*

discovered in 1974, is a large stone cross which was depicted by Lord Dunraven in 1871, but lost to the intervening generations.

The northern climb from Blue Cove is not nearly so steep and although it too is overgrown and dilapidated in patches, it is quite passable. At the bottom of this route, a section of about 50m has been enlarged by explosives – probably during the 1820 period of lighthouse construction.

Under present prevailing weather, a boat could use this north landing perhaps only ten days a year, so the fact that the monks undertook the

Fourteen steps to nowhere. Virtually inaccessible, these steps are carved from the solid rock, but they lead neither to the sea, nor the upper levels.

Old photograph taken in 1871, the monastic enclosure as it would have been during Lord Dunraven's visit.

Detail from the roof of Cell A. It is thought that the protruding stones were used as anchorages to secure protective sods or thatch.

giant task of constructing the stairway to this bleak cove is a good argument that weather conditions then were far better than now.

The south landing, by comparison, is quite useful and its lower steps below the roadway have been used and improved by the lighthouse authorities from time to time. But there is some mystery here too: carved into the solid rock face nearby are fourteen steps which are virtually inaccessible, stopping short at both ends and leading neither to the sea nor the higher levels! Another technical puzzle is this: how, and where (without the benefit and convenience of the modern road) did the monks keep their boats safely out of reach of the sea? A derrick here at Cross Cove, or an incredible amount of laborious manhandling are the only alternatives!

To reach the monastery today, one normally follows the lighthouse road from the landing point at Blind Man's Cove to a junction just beyond Cross Cove where the real ascent to the monastery begins via the old southern stairway of some 600 steps.

Access to the monastery terrace is by a tunnel in the retaining wall, and upon emerging within the shelter of this enclosure – some 100m x 30m – one finds the old stone dwellings and oratories huddled close together at various levels, almost as perfect as when first built.

'The scene is one so solemn and so sad,' says Lord Dunraven, 'that none should enter here but the pilgrim and the penitent. The sense of solitude, the vast heaven above and the sublime monotonous motion of the sea beneath would oppress the spirit, were not that spirit brought into harmony ...'

There are six corbelled, beehive-shaped huts and two boat-shaped oratories as well as many stone crosses and slabs, some graves, two wells – said to 'become dry in the case of cursing, swearing or blasphemy' – and the ruin of the medieval church. Tradition tells that there is also a deep subterranean tunnel leading away from the monastic site but although there are two features in the enclosure which could be associated with this idea, there is no clear evidence of any tunnel as such today.

The monastery huts are more or less rectangular in plan at floor

Opposite: The Small Oratory. Note that it is built on reclaimed ground which is supported by a substantial artificial terrace. The major work of installing a new foundation of concrete and stainless steel underneath the terrace was carried out in 1986.

The Small Oratory, Skellig Michael. Prior to the modern reconstruction.
(*PHOTO: OFFICE OF PUBLIC WORKS*)

level and take on a circular shape as the corbelling progresses upwards. We take them in the order in which one meets them.

CELL A

Cell A has a floor area of 4.5 x 3.8m and a height of 5m. The internal walls are almost straight to a height of 1.5m before the dome begins to narrow, and all around the interior of the walls at about 2.5m are protruding stone pegs which may have supported a wooden upstairs floor. The windows high up in the east and west walls would have given light at this level. On the exterior of the hut other stone pegs protrude and these may have been anchorages for protective sods or thatch. The door is 1.2 x 0.8m and the walls are 1.8m thick.

CELL B

Cell B is 2.7 x 2.7 x 3m high. There are two cupboard recesses in the internal walls, but no windows or protruding pegs inside or out. The door is 1.3 x 0.6m and the walls are 1.06m thick at the door.

Opposite:This square-shaped tower in the outer garden is a medieval toilet. Cell A is seen in the background.

CELL C

Cell C is 2.7 x 2.6 x 3.4m. It is quite like Cell B, being without windows or protruding stones. The door is also the same size.

CELL D

Cell D is only a ruin which may have been circular in plan. Its collapse is not of recent times.

CELL E

Cell E is very similar to Cell A. It also has the internal stone pegs on the walls. The floor, which is very well laid, is 3.6 x 3.5m, and the height is 3.9m. The door is 1.4 x 0.9m and the walls are 1.2m thick.

CELL F

It is thought that the roof of this cell collapsed between 1871 and 1891, and that the dome was reconstructed inaccurately, some 0.9m less than originally. This cell is now 2.5 x 2.7 x 3m. There are three cupboard recesses in the internal walls and again the internal stone pegs. The door is 1.2 x 0.6m and the walls are 1.1m thick at the door.

LARGE ORATORY

This building is boat-shaped with a door in the western wall. Its measurements are 3.6 x 2.4 x 3m. The stone altar which occupied the eastern wall was removed during the renovations of 1990. There is also a small window in this eastern wall.

SMALL ORATORY

This building is on a substantial artificial terrace some distance away from the group. It is 2.4 x 1.8 x 2.4m and there is a window, 0.6 x 0.3m in the north-eastern wall. The door is only 0.9 x 0.5m and the walls are 1m thick.

MEDIEVAL CHURCH

This is quite a ruin but its eastern window still stands. As distinct from the other buildings of the monastery, the construction of this medieval church contains imported stone – identified as coming from Reenadrolaun Point on Valentia Island – a feat of transport and labour which is almost incredible! In the centre of the church is a comparatively modern gravestone which refers to the lighthouse families of 1868, and was erected in this position some time after 1871.

Opposite: A cluster of beehive huts overlooks Small Skellig.

Skellig – a view from Valentia Island: Long Island and Horse Island occupy the middle ground, while Small Skellig (left) and Skellig Michael (right) stand on the horizon some eight sea miles (14km) offshore.

Adult gannets occupy Small Skellig from February – when they arrive to claim a nesting site – until late October.

Above: Fionán of Skellig *cruises past Small Skellig. The waters are deep, and boats can pass within an arm's length of the island to view the bird life in detail.*

Left: The Priest's Stone – tallest of Skellig Michael's many stone crosses, this monument dominates the settlement, especially the Monk's Graveyard.

Above: The Skellig Experience Visitor Centre on Valentia Island opened in 1992 and displays the wonders of Skellig – the Early-Christian monastery, the seabirds, the lighthouse service and the underwater life.

Framed in a disused doorway, the old North Station lighthouse of Skellig Michael.

Time for reflection – are these really stone crosses in the Monk's Graveyard or are they ancient Skellig monks turned to stone?

Skellig Michael (foreground) and Small Skellig: viewed from the west, the lighthouse becomes the focal point on Skellig Michael while the monastery buildings disappear.

White sea campion (foreground), white fulmar in the sky, monastic cells, and the vast seascape ... these beauties make up Skellig Michael's soul.

Skellig Michael's majestic domed buildings watch over the little stone crosses of the Monk's Graveyard.

The east window of Skellig Michael's medieval church – like every view from the monastery – looks out over sister-island Small Skellig just one sea mile (1.8km) away.

From a distance Small Skellig looks like an island of white marble. A closer look reveals that the marble consists of row upon row of snow-white gannets.

Puffins occupy Skellig Michael from April to early August. Late evening – when they congregate in large numbers – is the best viewing time.

Bristling now with modern electronics, the Skellig lighthouse still beams out the same basic light signals as it did in 1826.

The Lighthouse and its Men

Prior to 1820 there was no lighthouse between Cape Clear, County Cork, and Loop Head, on the Shannon – some 111 miles (179km) as the gull flies – of Ireland's fiercest coast. In 1820, on the request of Sir Maurice Fitzgerald, Knight of Kerry, approval for a lighthouse on Skellig Michael was granted. The Corporation for Preserving and Improving the Port of Dublin – predecessors of today's Commissioners of Irish Lights – bought the island from Butler of Waterville for the sum of £780, and engineer George Halpin was given a formidable construction task:

> To distinguish Skellig Michael from Loop Head or Cape Clear, and to ensure a wide arc of visibility, the plan called for two lighthouses on the rock – one at 53m above sea level near Seal Cove, and the other at 114m above sea level on the island's western extremity. As well as this, some 1000m of approach road had to be built from the landing place at Blind Man's Cove right out to the upper lighthouse at the opposite end of the rock, and clinging to the cliff face every inch of the way.

Desirable though the project was, some writers of the period were greatly alarmed by one aspect of the construction work. Butler, in his sale, had stipulated that the monastery buildings be carefully preserved, but it transpired that the road builders and lighthouse builders had been living in some of the monastery cells and using others for storing explosives. It is not clear how much the monastery suffered in this period, but other setbacks were noted:

> In December 1821, Mr Hill's sloop, *John Francis*, was burned off Portmagee while ferrying materials for the Skellig lighthouse construction. Mr Hill sought

compensation but the Board declined to pay! On 16 November 1825, one of the Skellig workmen, Peter Kane of Portmagee, was killed in a rock-blasting operation. His widow submitted a petition to the Board in the following February – and was awarded a pension of £6 per annum for herself and £3 per annum for each of her children under age sixteen.

However, by 1826, at a cost of £45,721, the two lighthouses were established, each showing a steady light from Argand oil lamps and parabolic reflectors, and each having two semi-detached houses close by, where the keepers and their wives and families resided for long periods of duty. Writing in 1837, Samuel Lewis reported:

> The erection of the lighthouses has been a means of preventing much loss of life and property. Scarcely a winter previously elapsed without frequent and fatal shipwrecks ...

One of the fatal Skellig shipwrecks to be recorded was the wreck of the *Lady Nelson*. Bound from Oporto to London with a cargo of wine and fruit, she struck the Skellig and went to pieces with the loss of all but three lives. Lady Chatterton wrote of the case in 1839:

> The mate had warned the captain during the evening of his proximity to this dangerous rock; but the captain, who was drunken and jealous, (his wife having seconded the representations of the mate), refused to put the vessel about and in a couple of hours she struck.
>
> The mate and three hands saved themselves upon a part of the wreck, which was drifting about for two or three days, during which time they subsisted on the oranges and other fruit which, when the ship went to pieces, covered the sea around them. The mate, who was an excellent swimmer, procured these oranges by plunging off the spar and bringing them to his companions. On the third day, one man became delirious; saying that he should go ashore to dine, he threw himself off the spar and sank.
>
> Shortly afterwards the survivors were picked up by

a fishing boat belonging to Dingle, which had come out looking for a wreck. The crew consisted of a father and his four sons, and had two pipes of wine in tow when they perceived the sufferers; finding their progress impeded by the casks and that the tide was sweeping the seamen into the breakers, where they must have been dashed to pieces, the old man nobly cut the tow line, abandoning what must have been a fortune to his family, and by great exertion picked the men up, just when the delay of a second would have caused their destruction.

The *Lady Nelson port* is still famous in Kerry, and a glass of it is sometimes offered as a 'bon bouche'.

What was life like at the Skellig lighthouses in those pioneer days? Perhaps there were good times but it is generally the hardship that is most remembered. Hugh Redmond of Wexford, one of the first Skellig lighthouse crew, lost both his sons and his nephew over the cliffs. John Sloane, writing in 1873, recorded in some detail that another of the early Skellig lighthouse men arrived there – and departed – in very unhappy circumstances indeed. Michael Wishart had been principal keeper on the Tuskar Rock lighthouse in 1820, when he and his assistant, Charles Hunter, became involved in a substantial smuggling enterprise.

'… A large cask and several small kegs of brandy up to 84 proof … and other excisable commodities.' Not only were they storing the goods on the Tuskar, but they made the mistake of sampling them so heavily that they were unable to light the lantern – which, of course, provoked deep inquiry. 'I gained the tower, and on entering it, found Hunter dead drunk on his back and Wishart in the same state on his side, they having Tapped the Admiral.'

On 23 October, 1821, Michael Wishart was demoted from his post of principal at Tuskar and later sent to Skellig as assistant, where he was killed by falling over the cliff while cutting grass for his cow.

It is easy to visualise such an accident on the steep slopes of Skellig. Even a century later Thomas Mason wrote:

> The lighthouse keepers have a couple of goats which are generally located in some almost inacces-

sible position at milking time. With bated breath I
have watched the men retrieve these perverse animals ... there is no place in the scheme of nature for
a giddy goat ...

But at least, it couldn't happen today because there are no goats,
and certainly no cows on the rock at present.

During 1845-46 'new technology' was tried at Skellig! Experiments
showed that rape seed oil was more suitable than the earlier sperm
oil, and consequently this new material was introduced generally into
the lighthouse service by 1848.

Wooden partitions were added to some of the Skellig lighthouse
bedrooms in 1862 'to give more privacy', but the inter-family privacy
between the two Skellig lighthouses must also have been in some
question, because in April 1865 the principal keeper of the lower
lighthouse was dismissed for having 'cruelly beaten up' the principal
keeper of the upper station!

In or about 1870, Thomas McKenna of Crookhaven was dismissed
from his post at Skellig lighthouse for being absent from duty when
the Commissioners made a surprise visit. But where had he been?
McKenna had gone exploring an underground tunnel in the monastery site but he ran into difficulty and was unable to get out.
Eventually, his plight was discovered and one of his companions also
entered the tunnel with a rope and brought McKenna to safety – but
not before the Commissioners had appeared on the scene, made their
feelings known and ordered that the entrance to the tunnel be closed
... Was this the underground tunnel of the earlier legend?

Another place with a story which is lost today because of rockfalls
in the area is Eliza's Corner – a spot on the roadway between the two
lighthouses which was named by Portmagee tradesmen who were
working on the rock over 100 years ago. Eliza Callaghan, after whom
the place was called, was a beautiful young woman who used to sit
out at this corner for hours on end knitting in the sunshine. But was
she a lighthouse daughter, much admired by the Portmagee men, or
was she the mourning mother of the two children, Patrick and William
Callaghan, who died in 1868 and 1869, aged two and three years, and
are buried in the medieval church ruin in the monastery? This is
something I may never know.

Joanie Cahill-O'Sullivan at Portmagee. She was a teacher to lighthouse children on Skellig, circa 1889.
(PHOTO: W. HARRINGTON)

One sad note which is recorded in the minutes of the lighthouse Board on 3 April 1869 is a letter from W. Callaghan, principal keeper of the lower Skellig lighthouse, 'requesting removal to another station, stating that he had buried two of his children on the island that another was lying ill ...' The request was noted by the inspector – but was not immediately carried out. Indeed, it must have been easy to die on Skellig in those days. Skellig visitor John Windele in 1851 also records a conversation with lighthouse man Rooney, who had 'lost a son by being clifted' at Seal Cove.

That other families with young children occupied Skellig about

*James Martin King – the last child to be born on Skellig on 30
October 1897.*

(PHOTO: V. KING)

1889 is also known, because the late Mrs O'Sullivan (1869-1963) of
Portmagee, formerly Miss Joanie Cahill, often recalled spending three
years of her youth on Skellig Michael as a teacher to the lighthouse
children.

And a final chapter in Skellig families was completed when James
Martin King, second son of Thomas and Mary King, was the last child
to be born on Skellig on 30 October 1897.

These distant parishioners were not exactly forgotten by the
mainland church – politically, at least. In 1889 the lighthouse Board
received a communication from the parish priest of Cahersiveen,

claiming that – in the interest of the Roman Catholic Church – the Skellig lighthouse keepers who, since 1880, had been appointed 'caretakers' of the Skellig monuments, should 'be of the Faith', and requesting that the present Protestant keepers be replaced! The Board ordered that 'the reverend gentleman be informed that they cannot accede to this request, but that every care is taken of the monuments'!

Finally, about 1900, a decision was taken to move the lighthouse mens' families to the mainland, and a block of eight dwelling houses (for Skellig and Inishtearaght families), was built on Valentia by Mr W.H. Jones of Dunmanway at a total cost of £7,570. Thus, Knightstown village took over from Portmagee which had been the Skellig shore base since 1820.

This is not to say that there was now some permanence of residence for the lighthouse men and their families. In fact the uprooting and many trans-Ireland gyrations continued – of which the various appointments of Thomas King, mentioned in an earlier paragraph, are typical:

> 1890, Inishtearaght, (Kerry)
> 1893, Ballycotton, (Cork)
> 1896, Skellig, (Kerry)
> 1899, Fanad Head, (Donegal)
> 1900, Inishtearaght, (Kerry)
> 1902, Rockabill, (Dublin)
> 1902, Bailey, (Dublin)
> 1906, Rockabill, (Dublin)
> 1908, Ballycotton, (Cork)
> 1912, Kinsale, (Cork)
> 1914, South Aran, (Galway)
> 1918, Arranmore, (Donegal)
> 1919, Wicklow Head, (Wicklow)
> 1923, Broadhaven, (Mayo)

The upper Skellig light was discontinued in 1866, and the lower light was altered to have a flashing character – which is still the means of distinguishing one lighthouse from another. In 1909 the latest type of paraffin vapour incandescent burner was installed as well as a new lens of dioptric type – that is to say, a lens made of a set of prisms placed around the light to focus it into a horizontal beam.

This lens also holds the secret of the flashing effect. The whole optical assembly revolves around a steady light source at a fixed speed and gives the impression of a flash as the beam swings through the observer's point of view.

On Michaelmas Day, 1902, a Portmagee seine-boat which had been fishing by the Skellig was wrecked at the island's landing while the crew were ashore for a rest. The sudden wind which had done the damage also prevented help from coming for a week. Meanwhile, the Skellig larder had thirteen extra mouths to feed and the marooned fishermen had ample time to reflect on the tradition that nobody goes fishing on Michaelmas Day ...

Further assistance to mariners was provided by Skellig lighthouse men in November 1916, and for their part in helping rescue two boatloads of survivors from the *S.S. Marina*, the three keepers were awarded £1 each from the Board of Trade and one guinea each from the *Marina's* owners.

World War II brought its share of conflict to the Skellig area. Dogged aircraft encounters and bombing of merchant vessels were frequent occurrences, but neutrality and security maintained a blanket of silence on such events.

One of the few incidents to be recorded – 5 March, 1941 – was the loss of an unidentified aircraft which crashed into the sea south of Skellig. But even that tale ended abruptly, because a subsequent search by the Irish Lights tender and the Fenit lifeboat yielded only an empty rubber life-raft. And the only Skellig-area war-incident to be thoroughly researched and published was the loss of an American Liberator bomber, VB-110-PB4Y-1, which hit Skellig Michael and crashed into the sea near the island's north face on 27 February 1944. (See Bibliography, *The Fatal Echo*.)

Explosive fog signals – four ounce charges, detonated electrically – were introduced at the Skellig in 1914. In 1936 Mason reported a gigantic explosion which occurred when an electrical fault detonated simultaneously some 300 of these explosive charges. 'It nearly lifted the island out of the sea,' but no harm ensued and this type of signal remained in use until 1953.

There was no fog at midnight on 18 November 1955 when the 90-ton French trawler, *Styvel*, ran headlong into the Skellig. She was heading home with a full cargo of fish when she hit the northern side of the rocks where the lighthouse cannot be seen. Luckily there was no loss of life. Although the *Styvel* began to sink immediately, Valentia lifeboat managed to tow her from the 80-metre depths of the Skellig to the comparative safety of Valentia harbour before she finally went down.

Had it happened a few years earlier, the outcome might have been different because December 1951 saw some of the worst weather that the Skellig has ever recorded. On 27 December a wave broke the glass of the lighthouse lantern – 53m above the sea – flooding the light and doing extensive damage. It was 3 January 1952 before a relief crew of fitters with new lighting equipment could be landed on the rock.

Bill Dumigan, now retired from the lighthouse service, recalls that Skellig accident:

> I was winding the light-machine when the lantern was smashed and I received a cut forehead from the broken glass ... During the storm we also lost our boat-landing and cargo derrick; all the stanchions leading to the landing were bent and the road was ripped away.

But worse tragedy was to hit Skellig lighthouse. On 22 August 1956, keeper Seamus Rohu was reported missing from Skellig. His comrades and other helpers searched the island over and over again. Valentia lifeboat and the lighthouse service vessel, *Valonia*, searched the sea around the rock for days, but all in vain.

By and large, the structure of the lower lighthouse remained as it was built in 1820 until quite recently. In 1964 the first step in a modernisation programme was taken with the installation of a powerful diesel derrick at Cross Cove, 42m above the sea, to be used for landing hundreds of tons of building materials. 1965 saw the beginning of the reconstruction. The two old dwellings were made into one and all the old interior plaster walls were studded and lined with a decorative plastic finish. A bedroom was provided for each keeper and two spare bedrooms for visiting tradesmen. An office was included for the principal keeper. A new bathroom with hot and cold water was installed and oil-fired central heating and electric power fitted throughout the building.

On 24 May 1966 a small temporary lantern with an electric flashing light was mounted on a nearby spur of rock, and the main light which had guided mariners for 146 years was extinguished. The old tower was swiftly demolished and shovelled into the sea, together with – regrettably – many old logbooks and allied papers which would be useful to researchers today! On the site was erected a new reinforced concrete tower, engine room and battery room, a workshop and an oil-pump room with a seven-year fuel supply. Instead of a paraffin vapour burner, a modern, three-kilowatt electric lamp was fitted, and the lens system of 1909, which was in perfect condition, was re-installed.

This new light, with its characteristic triple flash, its intensity of 1,800,000 candelas and its visible range of 27 miles (43km) came into operation on 25 May 1967. The total cost was £49,000.

Today's Skellig lighthouse is a far cry from the original, not alone in construction, comfort and equipment, but also, for instance, in transport. One remembers the industrious lighthouse relief boats – the 'old' *Ierne*, the *Deirdre*, the *Nabro*, the *Alexandra*, the *Valonia* and later the more sophisticated ships, the *Granuaile, Ierne, Isolda* and *Atlanta* – steaming around the coast on their lighthouse rounds.

One remembers the same ships weatherbound in harbour for days, perhaps weeks, while the Skellig men waited for relief and supplies. One remembers when emergencies arose at these moments to complicate the situation, and the many mercy dashes which Valentia lifeboat made to the Skellig lighthouse to bring injured men to safety. The station files tell the exciting events – but briefly:

> March 24th 1950: Lifeboat relieved Skelligs Rock. November 15th 1953: Assistant Keeper Gillian injured at Skellig. Landed by Valentia lifeboat. April 4th 1954, Captain Martin, Engineer of Irish Lights, ill on Skellig for seven days was taken ashore by Valentia lifeboat, after relief tender, *Valonia*, had failed to land in four attempts. June 15th 1963: Skellig keeper very ill. Taken off by Valentia lifeboat. October 25th 1965: Injured carpenter taken off Skellig by Valentia lifeboat …

All this changed in 1969. The Skellig dwellings on Valentia were closed; the lighthouse families moved away to live where they

Jim Lavelle – he built the Skellig bonfire in the emergency of 1936.

pleased, and a fortnightly helicopter service was inaugurated from Castletownbere to fly the lighthouse keepers to and from the Skellig pad in a matter of minutes.

Lighthouse communications too made great strides. Since 1970 the men on Skellig have had the normal telephone which is linked by VHF beam with the mainland exchange in Castletown, and make their calls like any other subscriber. Before this they had only the shipping-band radio-telephone for communication with other lighthouse establishments or with shipping or, in emergency, with Valentia Radio Station.

But before that, before the advent of radio to Skellig? They had semaphore signals. There was a large white-washed patch on the rock face beside the lighthouse road and a semaphore signaller standing in front of this could be read by telescope from the Bull Rock

The late Patrick 'Bonnet' O'Shea, who came to the assistance of the Skellig lighthouse emergency in 1936.

lighthouse – some 14 miles (22km) away – which, in turn, would relay the message ashore by similar means!

Two incidents highlight the difficulties of these early communications. In 1936, John Dore of Valentia, one of the three-man Skellig crew fell ill, but thick fog completely prohibited the normal semaphore communication with Bull Rock. Distress rockets were fired that night but of no avail. The fog persisted and the patient's condition grew worse.

The fog signal had to be manned by day. The light and the fog signal had to be maintained by night. Distress rockets had to be fired regularly and a watch had to be kept for the possibility of help from a passing boat or the chance of a clearance and a contact with the Bull Rock.

A second night passed and the rockets were finally exhausted –

without result. The patient was very ill, with only a basic first-aid box to succour him, and his two companions were still without sleep or even rest. What to do?

Every scrap of firewood, every box, packing case and provision basket, every newspaper, sack, rag and old uniform was carted manually, load by load, up the steep climb to the monastery pinnacle and a great bonfire was prepared. Oil from the lantern was drawn up the hill in gallons, tins, buckets and bottles and added to the fuel.

It was a whole day's work and as soon as darkness had fallen on the Skellig, assistant keeper Jim Lavelle set a match to his bonfire, sending flames roaring high into the air above the old monastery cells. The signal went far afield. A Portmagee fisherman, Patrick 'Bonnet' O'Shea, who saw the glow in the sky, understood the message and brought help in time.

Thirty-six years previously, during the fishing season of 1900, a similar fire had brought help in a similar situation. This time the Cahills' six-oar follower set out from Valentia to answer the distress, and although most details of the successful rescue are forgotten, the sequel to it is still told in Portmagee and Valentia: when the rescue boat landed in Portmagee after its 20 mile (32km) dash, the police sergeant stood in the doorway of the public house and refused to give the oarsmen admission because it was 'off hours'. Undaunted, they boarded their boat again and rowed the further five miles (8km) to Knightstown, where 'Galvin' gave them the freedom of the house.

Freedom of another house – the Skellig lighthouse – where for 160 years visiting boatmen and local friends would always receive a welcome fit for a king, where the kettle was always boiling – be it on the gas cooker of recent years or the coal fire of earlier days, where strong tea was always liberally dispensed, where friendship and the chat of kindred souls always flowed richly, passed into history on 20 April 1987, when the lighthouse was switched to fully automatic operation, unattended, unmanned, empty, locked up …

Seabirds of Skellig

If there is one facet of the Skellig lighthouse man's life which has not changed much in 150 years it is his interest in the lives and habits of nesting seabirds; and much of the ornithological literature of today received its early information from observant lighthouse men. Today, more than ever before, there is a growing appreciation of the Irish coast's wonderful natural treasure of birds – a treasure fast disappearing in other countries – and each year more and more students and observers are drawn here from far afield.

The Skellig rocks are Europe's ideal bird sanctuary. They are luckily situated far away from the pollution of city and industry, and luckily too, the birds of Skellig have never learned to fear man, and on this rock one can study from a range of a few metres, so many creatures which are never seen over the mainland.

The relative clumsiness of Skellig's seabirds, and the fact that they cannot take off from level ground but have to launch themselves from a ledge to become airborne, led to an early legend that some mysterious magnetism held the birds on the island. However, the terrestrial drawbacks are more than balanced by the great skill of the seabirds in the air and on – or beneath – the waves.

GANNET

Gannet – *Sula bassana*. Irish: *Gainéad;* French: *Fou de bassan;* German: *Basstölpel;* Swedish: *Havssula;* Dutch: *Jan van Gent.*

Pride of place in the bird life of the area must go to the gannet, which inhabits the Small Skellig rock to the relative exclusion of all other species. If there are some of the smaller seabirds on the lower ledges it is only because these perches do not offer enough space for the heavy, goose-sized gannets. Every other site on this precipitous 6.5 hectare, 135m crag is taken up by the 23,000 nesting pairs, which makes Small Skellig the second largest of the world's 23 gannet colonies.

First mention of the Small Skellig gannetry was in 1700. In 1748 the gannet population was 'an incredible number', and from then onwards the estimated figures fluctuated considerably.

1828 – 500 pairs
1880 – 30 pairs
1882 – 150 pairs
1906 – 15,000 pairs
1913 – 8,000 pairs
1941 – 10,000 pairs
1969 – 20,000 pairs

The gannet is obviously in a very strong position today, and one can only suggest that the fluctuations in the colony's early history were due to 'harvesting'. About 150 years ago, gannets were fetching 1s.8d. to 2s.6d. (7p–12½p) each, and as late as 1869 the Small Skellig was rented annually for the taking of feathers and young gannets. Indeed, high up on the south face of Small Skellig, hidden from passing boats, are the ruins of a man-made rectangular building which may have been a gannet-hunter's shelter... At breeding time the rock was guarded by a boat-crew of twelve men, 'well paid by the man who owned it', but this deterrent was inadequate, and Dunleavy – in Thomas O'Crohan's *The Islandman* – tells an exciting tale of one unauthorised gannet-raid which ended in bloodshed.

> This time a boat set out from Dunquin at night with eight men in her, my father among them, and they never rested till they got to the rock at daybreak. They sprang up it and fell to gathering the birds into the boat at full speed. And it was easy to collect a load of them for every single one of these young birds was as heavy as a fat goose. As they were turning the point of the rock to strike out into the bay, what should they see coming to meet them but the guard boat. They hadn't seen one another till that moment.

Then the activity began. The guards tried to take the Dunquin boatmen prisoners, but '... some of them sprang on board and they fell to hitting at one another with oars and hatchets, and any weapon they could find in the boat till they bled one another like a slaughtered ox.'

Although outnumbered by twelve to eight the Dunquin men won the fight and eventually got back to their own harbour with their boatload of gannets intact. When the vanquished guard boat reached its base, two men were dead, and the other ten were sent into hospital. 'After that they were less keen on that sort of chase and the guard was taken off the rock ...'

Even though the gannets do not lay until April or later, it seems that the nesting site is selected immediately on return from migration in February, and is guarded by one or other of the partners for the next six months. And this is hardly without reason. In a colony of 46,000 thieving neighbours, any unattended property, be it site, materials, nest, egg or chick, is unlikely to survive very long.

The gannet makes a large, high nest of weeds and all sorts of floating rubbish, and frequently the pursuit of these nest-building materials such as scraps of fishing net, ropes and twine, will result in entanglement and death – unless some kindly boatman happens to pass that way to put things right. Only one dull, greenish, white egg is laid. When hatched, the chick is snow-white but its true feathers are first black and later mottled, and it is not until the fourth year that the full adult plumage is attained – pure white with bold black wingtips and yellow head. The mature gannet is 0.9m in length, with a long neck, long pointed bill, pointed tail and long narrow wings. The wingspan is almost 1.9m.

First-year gannets migrate in November to the west coast of Africa or even in to the Mediterranean, but in successive years they travel much shorter distances, the older birds reaching only as far as the Bay of Biscay. One record traveller – a young gannet ringed on Small Skellig in 1968 was subsequently recovered on the coast of Brazil!

The gannet's flight is usually direct and low with frequent gliding, but while feeding it wheels high in the air and will plunge into the sea upon its prey from 30m or more. Evolution has designed the gannet well for this violent activity. It has no external nostrils, no real tongue, and has an intricate pneumatic system of air-cushion shock absorbers throughout its body.

The 'Changing of the Guard' at the nest when the gannet returns from a fishing trip is a highly ceremonious show – which is not confined just to breeding time. Both birds stand face to face, wings half open, bowing to each other and knocking their bills together with much contented grunting. No doubt it could be a very graceful affair if they had enough space, but in the crowded conditions of the Small Skellig, any protruding wingtip or tail which encroaches by an inch on a neighbour's territory is liable to provoke a sharp stab of retaliation which upsets the whole ceremony.

For two months the gannet chick remains in the nest, pampered and grossly overfed. Then it is deserted and it starves for two weeks before it plucks up the courage to take the plunge into the sea. If the young bird survives this first venture, it has a fair chance of living to an age of 40 years.

During his life the gannet will touch no other local area but his breeding station, and there is only one report of a gannet ever fishing inland – in an Antrim lake on a stormy day in 1932.

The Small Skellig, which is owned by Mr C. O'Connell of Dublin, has been leased by the Irish Wildbird Conservancy as an official seabird refuge, and studies still continue. On one July day in 1972, 671 young gannets were ringed and released.

PUFFIN

Puffin – *Fratercula arctica.* Irish: *Puifín*; French: *Macareux moine*; German: *Papageitaucher*; Swedish: *Lunnefågel*; Dutch: *Papegaaiduiker.*

The puffin, like the razorbill and the guillemot, is one of the auk family – black and white salt water divers with short, narrow wings and legs set far back. Their carriage is upright and their flight is fast and whirring, seldom for long in a straight line. All these birds use their wings to swim underwater, and they have been seen by aqualung divers as deep as 15m.

On Skellig Michael the puffins breed colonially in rabbit burrows or similar holes from which the rightful owners may be forcibly ejected. Only one egg is laid, round in shape and whitish in colour with light grey/brown spots. When the puffin chick is six weeks old it is deserted by the parents to fend for itself and to make its own way to sea.

Up to the beginning of this century puffins were captured in great numbers. Their plumage was a valuable article of trade and the young birds, well salted, were regarded as a delicacy. Two salted puffins could fetch a 'peck' of meal on the market.

The puffin is easily recognised: black plumage above, white below, grey cheeks and bright orange feet, but its bill is the most conspicuous feature. In winter this is dull yellow, and small, but in summer it is bright red, blue and yellow, laterally flattened and very strong. In appearance the puffin, which is 30cm in length, is stumpy and big-headed with an awkward shuffling gait. They are generally quiet birds, living from their underwater hunting, but when aroused or in a tussle over a nesting site they can fight fiercely.

At the end of March when the flocks of puffins arrive back at Skellig from their North Atlantic wanderings, they first swim around the rock for some days, not approaching very near. Then in the evening dusk a few – only a few – will venture ashore to spend the night. Finally in mid-April in the course of a couple of days the whole flock will settle on the island and take up residence. Skellig will now be over-run with puffins until the second week in August when, in response to some great unanimous decision, the puffins will depart as suddenly as they arrived.

RAZORBILL

Razorbill – *Alca torda.* Irish: *Crosán;* French: *Petit pingouin;* German: *Tordalk;* Swedish: *Tordmule;* Dutch. *Alk.*

The razorbill, 40cm in length, is black above with white underparts. The bill is almost black in colour, laterally compressed and has a conspicuous white line across the centre. The razorbill has a heavier head and shorter, thicker neck than the guillemot. It also looks more squat while swimming and generally carries its tail cocked up.

From March to August the razorbills are on the Skellig, although some early-comers return at the end of January – and the ledges below the road at the lighthouse are well-populated nesting sites.

One egg – a buff/blue colour, spotted with brown – is laid on the bare rock ledge without the benefit of any semblance of a nest, but, unlike the puffin, the razorbill tends its young for a long period even after the site has been abandoned. One conspicuous razorbill which retained its winter plumage in summer nested in the same spot on Skellig Michael for four years in succession.

GUILLEMOT

Guillemot – *Uria aalge*; Irish: *Forach*; French: *Guillemot de troil*; German: *Trottellumme*; Swedish: *Sillgrissla*; Dutch: *Zeekoet.*

The guillemot is an inoffensive bird and its eggs and young are a constant target for gulls and other predators. Black or very dark brown above, white below, the guillemot is 42cm in length. A slender, more pointed bill and a thinner neck distinguish it from the razorbill.

The guillemot makes no nest, but lays its single egg in mid-May on some inaccessible, crowded ledge above Seal Cove. The egg varies very much in colour from brown to green or white, blotched and streaked with brown, but its distinct pear shape cannot be mistaken. This shape too prevents the egg from rolling off its unprotected ledge.

An uncommon variation of this species – the Bridled Guillemot – with its distinctive white eye-stripe, has often been noted on the crowded ledges of Cross cove.

KITTIWAKE

Kittiwake – *Rissa tridactyla*; Irish: *Staidhséar*; French: *Mouette tridactyle*; German: *Dreizehenmöwe*; Swedish: *Tretåig mås*; Dutch: *Drieteenmeeuw.*

On Skellig Michael the kittiwake is the noisiest bird. It nests on the ledges above the landing, and at Cross Cove and Seal Cove, and seems to spend its summer screaming madly at the world at large. the voice is loud and clear and cannot be mistaken: 'kit-i-wake … kit-i-wake'.

The kittiwake is very much an open sea species which only once – in the year 1938 – has been seen inland. The wings and mantle are ash grey and the remainder of the plumage is pure white. It is distinguished from the common gull which is a similar size – 40cm in length – by solid black triangular wingtips, olive/brown legs, an unmarked, yellow bill and a dark eye.

The kittiwake generally returns to the Skellig in March – although the lighthouse records for 1972 show that some kittiwakes returned as early as 26 December – and its three eggs – stone coloured, spotted with grey and brown – are laid at the end of May. The kittiwake makes a sturdy nest of weeds and roots, and the largest Skellig Michael colonies are on the precipitous ledges of Cross Cove and Seal Cove – where the chicks are deserted to fend for themselves in August.

Infant mortality must be very high in these communities. Fights between adults on the narrow ledges frequently result in eggs or chicks being hurled over the edge and into the sea, where those predators, the herring gull and the black-backed gull, are ever watchful for an easy meal!

STORM PETREL

Storm petrel – *Hydrobates pelagicus*. Irish: *Mairtíneach*; French: *Pétrel tempête*; German: *Sturmschwalbe*; Swedish: *Stormsvala*; Dutch: *Stormvogeltje*.

At 15cm in length, the storm petrel is the smallest European seabird, visiting land only while breeding. It is sooty black, with a conspicuous white rump and a square black tail.

There is a large breeding colony of storm petrels on Skellig Michael but they are seldom seen by day as they remain hidden in their nests or else far out to sea. At evening time they appear, flitting just above the waves, feet dangling so low that they appear to be running on the water.

They return to the Skellig at the end of April, and by the end of June one oval egg – white, with rust spots – is laid in a burrow, under a stone, or deep within the stonework of the old monastery buildings with little or no nesting material. Incubation takes 5 or 6 weeks and during this time the bird will often wander great distances for food, leaving the egg or the chick unattended for days.

Occasionally the voice of the storm petrel – a purring sound with a 'hiccough' at the end – will lead you to its nest. But beware. This bird can spit out an evil-smelling oil with great accuracy if interfered with. The storm petrel, also known as Mother Carey's Chicken takes to the open sea again in October. They are never seen inland – except after some fierce storms in 1839 and 1891 when these birds were strewn dead over miles of countryside.

MANX SHEARWATER

Manx shearwater – *Puffinus puffinus*. Irish: *Cánóg*; French: *Puffin des anglais*; German: *Schwarzschnabel – Sturmtaucher*; Swedish: *Mindre lira*; Dutch: *Noordse Pijlstormvogel*.

The manx shearwater is very clumsy on land and is seldom seen there by day. Even on fine, calm nights they prefer to hide away, and it is only on cloudy, windy nights when the shearwaters venture out in their full force and full voice, that an idea of the local population can be formed.

They are sometimes seen in groups, particularly towards evening time when large flocks gather on the water near the breeding ground.

Sooty black above, white underneath and 35cm in length, the shearwater is recognised easily by its distinctive flight – very low over the sea, following the contours of each wave, gliding frequently on stiff wings with only occasional wing beats.

In March the shearwaters return from their winter migration in South America. They breed in burrows and will use the same burrow year after year. One white, oval egg – very large in relation to the bird – is laid at the end of April and both birds sit, but frequently the nest is left unattended for days while the birds forage far afield for food.

In the summer of 1972 one shearwater had her nest at the foot of the altar steps in the old oratory of the Skellig monastery. Indifferent to visitors and cameras she sat for the prescribed time, but she must have moved to some more secluded site as soon as the chick arrived because from then on we saw her no more.

Parenthood is a long task for the shearwaters. Incubation takes $7\frac{1}{2}$ weeks, and the chick remains in the nest for a further $10\frac{1}{2}$ weeks, by which time it has become far heavier and fatter than the parent birds. Eventually it is deserted and suffers a week's starvation before it decides to venture forth to the sea. And this big initial adventure must be made under cover of darkness. The young shearwater is so helpless on land that it would be promptly devoured by gulls if it showed itself by day.

FULMAR

Fulmar – *Fulmarus glacialis*. Irish: — French: *Pétrel glacial;* German: *Eissturmvogel;* Swedish: *Stormfågel;* Dutch: *Noordse Stormvogel.*

Before the year 1900, the fulmar was a rare visitor to Ireland from Northern regions, but its numbers and breeding stations were rapidly spreading southwards, and in 1913, R.M. Barrington reported 12 pairs

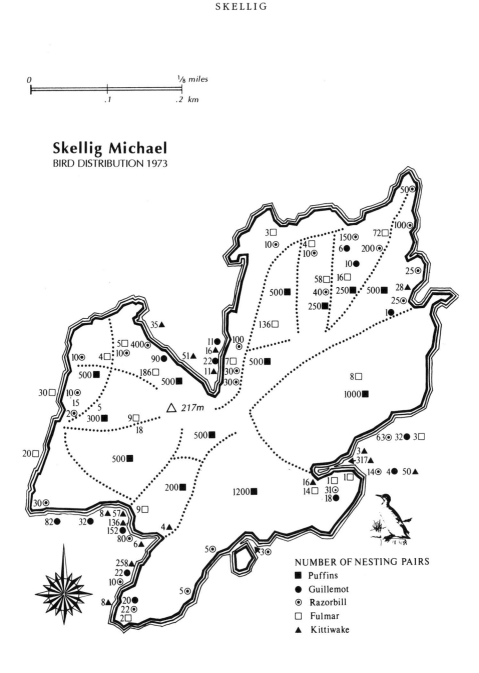

0   ⅛ miles

.1   .2 km

Skellig Michael
BIRD DISTRIBUTION 1973

NUMBER OF NESTING PAIRS

■ Puffins
● Guillemot
⊙ Razorbill
□ Fulmar
▲ Kittiwake

Seabirds of Skellig
(numbers of nesting pairs)

BIRDS	SKELLIG MICHAEL			SMALL SKELLIG
	1969	1973	1990	1969
Gannet				20,000
Puffin	6000	6000	2237	
Razorbill		750	86*	35
Guillemot		250	266	575
Kittiwake		950	1031	1120
Storm Petrel	1000 TO 10,000	1000 TO 10,000		
Manx Shearwater	1000 TO 10,000	1000 TO 10,000		
Fulmar		588	482	10
Herring Gull	250	129	25	
Lesser Black Back		28	40	
Greater Black Back	12	6	4	

* The low count may have been exaggerated by the late date of the survey: 14th July

nesting for the first time on Skellig Michael. Some 70 birds arrived in 1914, and about 100 in 1915. Thus the colony was established and from Skellig they spread out to other local rocks and cliffs.

The fulmar finally found peace in this period and this area. Only thirty years previously some 12,000 fulmars were 'harvested' annually on St. Kilda alone – 115 birds per every member of the population. One report put it this way: 'No bird is of such use. The fulmar supplies oil for their lamps, down for their beds, a delicacy for their tables, a balm for their wounds and a medicine for their distempers...'

The fulmar is gull-like in appearance, 50cm in length, with a white head and a grey back, wings and tail. But here the similarity ends. The fulmar has a thick neck, a short, hooked, yellow bill with conspicuous tubed nostrils, and a distinctive, stiff-winged flight with wonderful mastery of air currents.

The fulmars are at Skellig from January to September. They nest at all levels, frequently in easily-accessible places among the tussocks of flowering sea pink, both parents taking four-day duty tours incubating the single white egg which is enveloped completely in underfeathers. Easily accessible, yes, but the fulmar will eject mouthfuls of foul-smelling oil at any curious intruder who comes too near.

Fulmars seen for the first time in a new area are not necessarily nesting; it is their habit to 'prospect' a cliff very thoroughly for a few seasons before deciding to breed there.

OTHER SPECIES

There are ravens on Skellig and there are hooded crows; there are wheatens and wrens and choughs and rock pipits, oystercatchers and shags, herring gulls and black-backed gulls, all of which can also be found commonly on any nearby mainland cliff or beach. In spring and autumn, one can be lucky and sight many interesting migrating species from other regions – skuas, knots, great shearwaters, turnstones, phararopes ... but not one of these has quite the same magic as the island's truly oceanic natives, who live and die on the endless ocean, coming ashore here only of necessity to reproduce their own kind.

Geology and Plants

It is difficult to imagine that these isolated crags now surrounded by seas which are 80m deep, were once part of a great mainland peninsula – but this seems to be so. The 350 million-year-old red sandstone and green and purple slate of Skellig are identical to the adjacent mainland even in general direction and dip.

Several major cracks or faults occur in Skellig Michael and these are particularly noticeable at sea level where they penetrate the rock as caves. All of these fissures have been entered and probed in recent years and while the caves at Blind Man's Cove and Cross Cove run for less than 50m the openings under the lighthouse at Seal Cove, and under the north landing at Blue Cove are long interesting caverns which still hold most of their secrets.

Geology leads to botany and here a whole new aspect of Skellig opens up. Reading Crofton Croker's reports of a century-and-a-half ago, one must assume that he was not very accurate in his observations when he said: 'Verdure there was none to soothe the eye of the weary pilgrim; all was nakedness and barren rock …' One can still generalise and say that the vegetation of Skellig is rather sparse, but this is not entirely true; there are thirty-eight species of hardy rock plants on Skellig Michael, which, in season, bloom from April onwards, providing patches of splendid greenery and colour.

All Skellig plants are rather common species – found in any seacliff terrain – and there is nothing which would relate directly to the earlier monastic cultivation. Although some of these common cliff plants could still supplement a basic monastic diet to some advantage, in legend only do we find reference to a miraculous crop of corn – and a miraculous supply of provisions which saved the monks from starvation until the corn could be harvested!

The most conspicuous – and puzzling – recent development in the flora of Skellig Michael is the fact that large areas of sea pink are dying out. The whole southern face of the island which up to 1970 was a firm stronghold of the sea pink and rock sea spurrey, has become

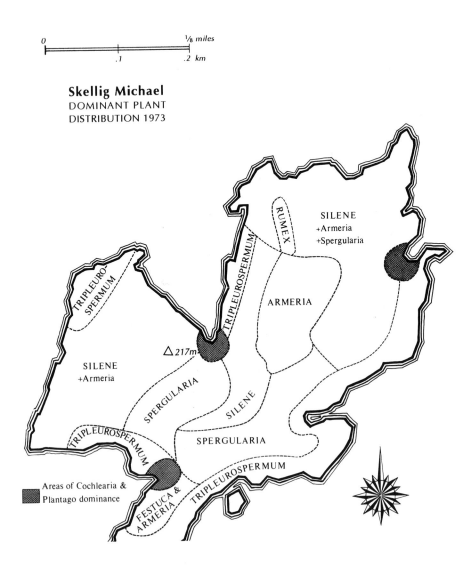

Skellig Michael
DOMINANT PLANT
DISTRIBUTION 1973

0   ⅛ miles
.1   .2 km

SILENE
+Armeria
+Spergularia

RUMEX

TRIPLEUROSPERMUM

TRIPLEUROSPERMUM

ARMERIA

TRIPLEURO-
SPERMUM

SILENE
+Armeria

△ 217m

SPERGULARIA

SILENE

TRIPLEUROSPERMUM

SPERGULARIA

TRIPLEUROSPERMUM

Areas of Cochlearia &
Plantago dominance

FESTUCA &
ARMERIA

Plants of Skellig

Agrostis stolonifera	Creeping bent	June-Aug.
Agrostis tenuis	Common bent	July-Aug.
Aira Praecox	Early hair grass	April-June
Anagallis arvensis	Scarlet pimpernet	June-Aug.
Armeria maritima*	Sea pink	March-Sept.
Asplenium marinum	Sea spleenwort	
Atriplex glabriuscula	Babington's orache	July-Sept.
Atriplex hastata*	Hastate orache	Aug.-Sept.
Beta vulgaris*	Sea beet	July-Sept.
Cerastium fontanum	Common mouse-ear	April-Sept.
Cerastium tetrandrum	Dark green chickweed	April-Oct.
Cirsium vulgare	Spear thistle	July-Sept.
Cochlearia officinalis*	Common scurvy grass	May-Aug.
Dryoptens dilatata	Buckler fern	
Festuca rubra	Red fescue	May-June
Holcus lanatus	Yorkshire fog	May-Aug.
Jasione montana	Common sheep's bit	May-Aug.
Juncus bufonius	Toad rush	
Leontodon autumnalis	Smooth hawkbit	July-Oct.
Plantago coronopus*	Buck's-horn plantain	May-Aug.
Plantago maritima	Sea plantain	June-Aug.
Poa annua	Annual meadow grass	All year
Poa trivialis	Rough meadow grass	June-July
Polypodium vulgare	Common polypody	
Rumex acetosa	Common sorrel	May-June
Rumex crispus	Curled dock	June-Oct.
Sagina maritima	Sea pearlwort	May-Sept.
Sagina procumbens	Common pearlwort	May-Oct.
Sedum anglicum	English stonecrop	June-Aug.
Senecio jacobaea	Ragwort	June-Aug.
Silene maritima*	Sea campion	June-Aug.
Sonchus asper	Prickly sowthistle	June-Aug.
Sonchus oleraceus	Common sowthistle	June-Aug.
Spergularia rupicola*	Rock sea spurrey	June-Sept.
Stellaria media	Chickweed	All year
Trifolium repens	White clover	May-Oct.
Tripleurospermum maritimum*	Scentless chamomile	July-Sept.
Umbilicus rupestris	Wall pennywort	June-Aug.

*Plants also found on Small Skellig

more denuded and has been eroded to an alarming degree. Botanists do not have an explanation for this, but far-reaching effects may well result from the change, because the tough root systems of the pinks were the main reinforcement for much of the soil on the island's steep slopes.

Small Skellig has not been extensively studied for plant life, and although very little greenery is evident to the casual observer, the eight species reported in the plant-lists may not really be the complete picture.

Skellig Sea World

Passing near Skellig by boat, one cannot miss the island's grey seals (*Halichoerus grypus*). They spend their summer days basking on the rock ledges or fishing adroitly in the surrounding seas.

Fifty was the greatest number of grey seals I have ever seen on the rocks at the one time and that was in mid-September 1989. One big, conspicuous bull seal – with that characteristic, humped nose – occupied the highest position in the herd, and many, straight-nosed expectant female greys, only a few weeks away from pupping time, lay about nearer the water's edge.

How convenient that it is by their noses – the only part which is visible as they swim – that seals are identified. Had there been any of Ireland's other seal, the common seal (*Phoca vitulina*) in the area, their pert, upturned noses would have been their identification.

Seals are inquisitive creatures, as has often been noted by aqualung divers in the area. Swimming up close to a diver, the seals will stare at him in what appears to be stark, wide-eyed disbelief, and then dash away again – only to repeat the performance a moment later. One wonders if they would be so entertaining and playful at the end of September when their new, white 13kg pups have arrived.

One wonders too, at a time like this if there is any justice for Ireland's 2000 grey seals and their annual 460 pups. Seals are a protected species, and any person who has ever sailed near the Small Skellig on a fine day and drifted a while to study the sleek, grey bewhiskered forms, or anyone who has found that he himself is under close scrutiny as another big-eyed, wide-nostrilled, black head pops up a few metres away from the boat, will feel that there must be ways of protecting salmon stocks other than the incessant killing of these beautiful beasts on various other parts of our coast.

For those of us who have the opportunity to extend our exploration of Skellig to the underwater world, there is much reward. The seals, the giant, harmless basking shark, the shoals of pollack and mackerel, the defiant lobsters, the proud crawfish and the rich colours of the anemone-clad rock faces, create a silent moonscape of remarkable beauty. The whims of wind, weather and tide add to the infinite variety of this area, and it is little wonder that in the short space of years since aqualung diving has become a popular sport, the name of Skellig has become famous in the diving circles of Europe.

Skellig is a place for experienced divers only. Its underwater cliffs plunge downward in sheer, vertical faces to a depth of 70m where they finally become part of that gently sloping, rock-strewn plateau which is the Continental Shelf, and many factors other than the capacity of one's air cylinders govern the time which may be spent admiring the underwater world.

Depth (pressure) and time impose a very exact limit to the amount of diving one can do in a day, and to exceed this limit is to court death or crippling disablement from 'the bends'. Cold is another factor. Skellig waters are well tempered by the Gulf Stream but even though the surface temperature may be 16ºC. on a summer's day, the layers 30m down may be as low as 10ºC. Notwithstanding the efficient insulation of modern diving suits, such cold can ultimately bring many attendant hazards.

Visitors who come to Skellig for its archaeology or ornithology frequently view divers with some perplexity when these black-suited figures slip into the sea and disappear in a trail of bubbles. 'What on earth are they looking for?' is the immediate question.

The answer is complex, and perhaps one needs to be a diver to appreciate it. Here, lapping our own shore, is a world as alien as the moon, yet full of life, full of history, possibly full of indications for the future – just waiting to be explored. We can learn from it; we can live from it; if we came from it, perhaps we can go back to it some day. There is a new maturity of thought in the diving world; the speargun has been rejected; the underwater cameras, with light meters, flash equipment and all the trappings of successful photography, have been embraced by many for an orderly, intelligent approach to a new frontier.

It was a quirk of Skellig weather which led three Limerick divers to an interesting find in the spring of 1975.

Opposite: The razorbill builds no nest, but lays her one large egg on an open ledge. Exposed and vulnerable, this egg must be constantly guarded against predators such as the herring gull.

A small sample of the island's gannet colony of 23,000 pairs sits on the north-east cliff of Small Skellig. In the background the headlands of Ducalla and Bolus on the mainland are visible.

Recent counts of Skellig razorbills have shown quite a decrease – as yet it is uncertain whether this is a natural fluctuation or a longterm decline.

The puffins on Skellig have little fear of visitors, each can study the other from only a metre or two away!

Nesting fulmars on Skellig have an unfriendly defence tactic – they can spit a foul-smelling oil at intruders from a range of five or six metres!

*Gannets on the wing can spot a fish from a height of up to 60 metres
and dive for their prey with pinpoint precision.*

On Skellig, kittiwakes nest on the most precipitous ledges. Three eggs are laid but in such hazardous locations, only one chick, sometimes two, ever survives.

The Skelligs have a resident population of about 50 grey seals. Their frequent sun-bathing may give the impression of laziness, but in fact they often swim 20 or 30 miles (32 to 48km) offshore to fish.

The cuckoo wrasse, normally found at a depth of about 98 feet (30m), is one of Skellig's most colourful fish. Curious by nature, it will venture quite close to divers and offers good photo opportunities. (PHOTO: JOS AUDENAERD)

Brilliant jewel anemones in every colour carpet the underwater rockfaces of Skellig.
(PHOTO: PAUL BURTON)

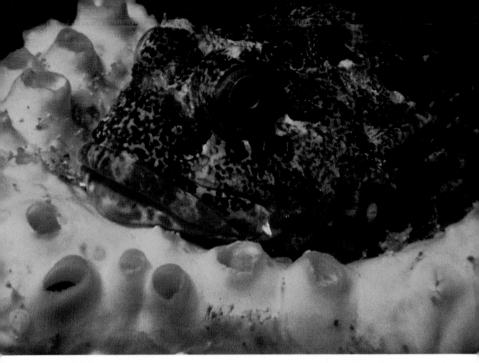

The scorpion fish of Skellig waters is not as dangerous as its name suggests!
(PHOTO: BILLY RAFTER)

Jewel anemones in fuchsia and purple provide a striking contrast to sagartia in brilliant white in Skellig's underwater world.

John, Martin and Noel are on board the diving boat *Béal Bocht.*
The wind is north-east, Force 4, which means that they must dive on
the west side of the islands. Small Skellig, with its interesting seal
coves, is the choice.

Experienced divers, they kit up with the full array of equipment:
suit, life jacket, aqualung, weight belt, knife, watch, depth gauge,
compass, fins, mask, snorkel ... Lamp in hand, they slip over the side
and are gone.

Down the steep rock-face they glide, swimming through a 3m high
forest of gold and red weed. The yellow colours begin to disappear
as they descend, then the reds. There is still ample light, and
horizontal visibility is 12m or more, but gradually everything becomes
blue. The divers switch on their lamps to compensate for this colour
filtration, and immediately all the glorious red and yellow sponges
and the green and turquoise anemones come back to vivid life.

It is silent here. The only audible sound is the two-tone hiss of
respiration and exhaust bubbles. A seal swims into view, grey and
ghostly, and suddenly is gone again − totally masterful in his own
environment.

At 25m, the seaweed begins to thin out and only a few barren
stalks remain. A shoal of pollack passes overhead, reducing the weak
daylight to almost nil. The divers pause and watch the intricate,
army-like movements of the shoal: 'Left turn. Right turn.' To some
unheard command, ten thousand fish turn as one, synchronised to a
fraction of a second. 'About turn. Slow march.' The shoal moves on ...

Now the divers are in the bottom of a gully, 30m below the surface;
there is little or no weed growing at this depth and the surrounding
water is deathly still − but it is a deceptive stillness; the smooth polish
on the rock face is indicative of the savage abrasions of sand and
boulders during winter storms.

A spotted dogfish − lazy offshoot of the shark family − lumbers
into the scene and flops down on a flat rock for a rest. Bleary-eyed
and lethargic in appearance, he is reluctant to be disturbed, and even
when the divers swim up close to study him he moves on only a few
metres, and rests again.

From the dim cavern beneath a large boulder, the cold, baleful
stare of a conger eel is fixed on the three approaching newcomers.

Steel-blue body, white mane erect along the length of his back, the conger is powerful, fearsome and sinister – but he tends to mind his own business if he is left unmolested.

A huge angler fish, perfectly camouflaged in his grey mottling, lies on the shingle between the rocks, his mouth – almost as wide as his body is long – wide agape. His 'fishing rod' dangles from his nose as a bait to entice smaller fry within range of his razor-sharp teeth. He is another one best left alone!

A colourful green scorpion fish rests on a bed of brilliant yellow sponge, offering a splendid photo opportunity.

The divers continue along the crevasse, checking time and depth frequently. Here is a lobster in resplendent blue, aggressive and unafraid; he raises his claws and challenges the intruders. There in the shelter of an overhanging ledge is a fragile rose-coral in muted apricot. Here is a crawfish in sunset red, clinging to a pointed crag. He shoots off backwards out of sight with a few powerful thrusts of his tail. Left or right, up or down, an indescribable variety of colour blazes on every side when touched by the pencil beam of the lights.

The three companions stop, rock-still, hardly breathing. Here is an ancient anchor and some fragments of rusted chain – and a cannon – and some lead pipes – and another cannon – and another ... A wreck at the Skellig! What ship was this? When was it lost? What hardship and misery did these sailors suffer in their final hours, with only the wild Atlantic for a grave, the gaunt rocks for a headstone, and the ever-screaming gannets for a dirge?

In the boat, we have been following the progress of the divers' bubbles, and finally the three men surface right beside our boarding ladder. 'Cannons and anchors and lead plumbing ...' They are agog with the news even before they climb out of the water. 'The cannons are about 2.5m in length ... the lead pipe is about 10cm in diameter the anchors are long and have strange-shaped flukes ...' It seemed like a big joke or a dream, and we were not quite prepared to believe that after some ten years of diving and exploration in this area, the Skellig had finally yielded an unknown wreck!

The temptation was great. Everyone wanted a cannon for his front lawn ... and the lead pipe would have good value as scrap ... But a different policy was adopted. A small sample of the lead was lifted

'The Wailing Woman' stone on Skellig Michael gazes towards Small Skellig and the distant South Kerry mainland.

for chemical analysis and to photograph a rather ornate plumber's joint. One cannon ball was removed for preservation, and for the duration of the summer's diving in the area, the motto was 'search and report'.

It will take more summers at Skellig before anyone can determine the extent or the significance of this site, but preliminary pointers suggest a small vessel of the 18th or 19th century, and it is possible that we are looking at the resting place of that 97 ton, single-decked brig, constructed by Capt. and Co. at Lowestoft in 1802, owned and skippered by Mr J. Sterry, last surveyed in 1834, registered in London and named *The Lady Nelson*.

I'm not sure that I really want to know for certain. For me it is exciting to have one more Skellig question which does not have a concrete answer.

A Hundred Years from Now

Such are the Skellig rocks – Skellig Michael and Small Skellig – not our properties but nonetheless our individual and collective responsibilities.

What does fate hold for these islands, as a new millennium dawns? Can the ancient buildings, which braved the Viking attacks and weathered fifteen hundred years of Atlantic storms, survive an ever-increasing tourist traffic, and go unscathed? Or will the same uneasy Atlantic be a limiting factor – a safety valve – to the number of visitors which Skellig can receive in any one year?

Stone cross carved from the solid rock, Skellig Michael.
(PHOTO: OFFICE OF PUBLIC WORKS)

The more immediate question is: can the ancient stonework – particularly the monastic site and the access stairways – survive the depredations of the island's rabbits? Assuming that these animals are a relatively recent importation to Skellig – possibly in the lighthouse era – already their burrowing has precipitated such rockfalls that the lighthouse road near Cross Cove has had to be roofed for safety, and the road to the upper lighthouse has long since been closed for the same reason. One shudders to think of the example of Church Island in Valentia harbour, where rabbits undermined and destroyed other old buildings in a short period of time.

Be it related to the rabbits, or otherwise, the death of the plant cover and the severe erosion on the south face of the island is a major cause for concern – not least because the island's only access road, clinging to the cliff face, is at the base of this slope, and will be at the receiving end of major rockfalls sooner or later.

The Office of Public Works – the nation's guardian of Skellig archaeology – was guilty of much neglect of the island for exactly 100 years, and guilty of much tardiness in relation to Skellig masonry falls even in 1972. Eventually, like a slow-moving pendulum, it swung in 1978 to the happy medium of steady maintenance, then to the other extreme of major reconstruction and cliff-top repair work involving the total exclusion of the public from the island during 1986! In this context, in May 1986, two massive stone pillars were erected on the roadway near the landing place, and two great, locked, insurmountable steel gates conveyed a certain finality to the long-trodden route of pilgrim and appreciative Skellig visitor. In November 1986, nature restored the status quo when a great storm swept every vestige of gates and pillars into the ocean without trace!

Will there be another round in this contest? I think so. But next time the Lighthouse Authority will not be a front-line player, having sold Skellig Michael to the Office of Public Works in 1987 ...

And what of the much-mentioned and confused regulations relating to small-boat transport of Skellig visitors – partly administered heretofore by the County Council under the Public Health (Amendment) Act, 1907, now administered by the Department of the Marine under the Merchant Shipping Act, and riddled throughout with antiquated and inappropriate legislative components? Will this sub-

Cells A (left), B and C, Skellig Michael, prior to the modern restoration work. The foreground terrace presents a rather different appearance today.

ject, vital to the Skellig itself and to the whole tourist industry, ever be reviewed, brought up-to-date and put into a manageable, logical format? It is time.

What of the birds? Will they always be safe, unmolested, unpolluted in their Skellig island sanctuaries? Dare we hope or presume that the name of Skellig will never be linked with such environmental horror-words as Torrey Canyon, Betelgeuse, Amoco Cadiz, Exxon Valdez …?

And what of the Skellig lighthouse service? A decade ago, this employment seemed as permanent as the old red sandstone itself, yet suddenly everything fell victim to economics and automation, as electronic ghosts behind steel doors now mindlessly light the Skellig

Opposite: Slabs and crosses in the Monk's Graveyard.

lantern at dusk, and extinguish it at dawn. No more the friendly, white-capped, brass-buttoned figure down at the landing place to greet and help the visiting boatman on a summer's day; no more that skilled, observant Skellig father-figure, watching over mariners in distress in winter, listening, reporting, assisting ... This is not progress; it is a backward step of 160 years.

But these are only the little affairs of men. The real Skellig survives, its body of living stone and its totally indescribable soul reincarnated annually in the beautiful form of puffins and petrels and gannets and fulmars and sea pinks and seals and sharks and whales and dolphins and summer skies and shining silver seas.

This is a permanent portion of heaven, too wonderful to lock up, too precious to neglect, too tender to tamper with, and crying out for a real Solomon who can wisely chart its future course. Those who have known Skellig intimately in the past are honoured; those who shall be lucky enough to see Skellig in the future must not take their pleasure lightly, nor shirk their undeniable responsibilities to this place.

Bibliography

The Skelligs and many aspects of these two islands are reported in various languages and many publications too numerous to mention. These are my principal and most useful references:

Ancient History of the Kingdom of Kerry, by Friar O'Sullivan of Muckross Abbey, ed. by Fr. J. Prendergast (J. Cork H.A.S. 1900), pp. 152 ff.

Annals of Innisfallen, ed. Sean Mac Airt (1951) pp. 124-25, 136-37, 208-09.

Annals of the Kingdom of Ireland by the Four Masters, ed. O'Donovan, pp. 666-67.

Annals of Ulster, ed. W. Hennessey, vol. I, pp. 318-10.

Antiquarian Handbook, R.S.A.I., 1904, ed. R. Cochrane.

Charlesworth, *The Geology of Ireland*, Oliver & Boyd, 1953.

Chatterton, *Rambles in the South of Ireland*, vol. I, 1839. Publ: Saunders & Otley.

De Paor, *A Survey of Sceilig Mhichil*, J.R.S.A.I., 1955.

De Paor, *Early Christian Ireland*, Thames & Hudson, 1960.

Donaldson, *The Fatal Echo*, Warplane Research Group of Ireland, 1990.

Dunraven, *Notes on Ir. Arch.*, vol. I (ed. by M. Stokes), George Bell & Sons, 1875.

Fisher, *The Fulmar*, London Collins, 1952.

Fisher and Vevers, *The Journal of Animal Ecology, Nos. 11, 12*, 1943.

Foley, *The Ancient and Present State of the Skelligs, Blasket Islands, etc.*, 1903.

Giraldus Cambrensis, *In Topographia Hibernie* ed. J. O'Meara.

Hayward, *In the Kingdom of Kerry*, 1946.

Henry, *Early Monasteries, Beehive Huts and Dry-stone Houses*, Proc. R.I.A.,

Horn, White-Marshall & Rourke, *The Forgotten Hermitage of Skellig Michael*, University of California Press, 1990.

Jackson, *Scéalta ón mBlascaod*, An Cumann le Béaloideis na hEirinn.

J.R.S.A.I. 1892, J. Romilly Allen, pp. 277 ff.

Keating, *History of Ireland*, vol. I, lines 1342-46; vol. III, 1.2480.

Keeble Martin, *The Concise British Flora in Colour*, Michael Joseph.

Kennedy, *The Birds of Ireland*, Oliver & Boyd.

La Croix, *John Paul Jones*, Muller, 1962.

Lewis, *Topographical Directory of Ireland*, 1837.

Lockley; *The Irish Naturalist's Journal, Vol. 15, No. V*, 1966.

Martyrology of Tallaght, (Henry Bradshaw Society, vol. LXVIII).

Matthews, *British Mammals*, Collins, London.

Maxwell, *A Book of Islands*, Bell & Sons, London, 1945.

McClintock, *Old Irish and Highland Dress*, Dundalgan.

Morris, *A History of British Birds*, (8 vols.), Groombridge.

Newman J.H. *Historical Sketches, III* – Longmans, 1917.

O'Crohan, *The Islandman*, Talbot, 1937.

ODonoghue, *Brendaninia*, 1870.

O'Gorman, *Breeding Stations of the Grey Seal*, Bulletin Mamm. Soc., 1963.

O'Kelly, P.R.I.A. Vol 59.C.2. 1958.

O'Rourke, *The Fauna of Ireland*, Mercier.

Peterson, *A Field Guide to the Birds of Britain and Ireland*, Collins, 1966.

Praeger, *The Botanist in Ireland*, Hodges & Figgis, 1934.

Praeger, *The Natural History of Ireland*, Dundalk, 1950.

Praeger, *The Way That I Went*, Allen Figgis, 1969.

Reade, *Nesting Birds*, Blandford.

Scully, *Flora of County Kerry*, Hodges & Figgis, 1916.

Seamus Dubh, ed., *The Songs of Tomas Ruadh O'Sullivan*, Gill, 1914.

Smith, *The Ancient and Present State of the County Kerry*, 1756.

Westropp, Proc. R.S.A.I. 1897, p.308-135.

Wilson, *The Irish Lighthouse Service*, Allen & Figgis, 1968.

Wynne, *Geological Survey of Ireland*, H.M.S.O., 1861.

DANCES WITH WAVES: AROUND IRELAND BY KAYAK

Brian Wilson

Brian Wilson is one of the few people to circumnavigate Ireland by kayak and this is the story of his voyage of 1200 gruelling miles along a beautiful and often hazardous coastline. He encountered adventures on land and sea – kidnapped and ransomed on Sherkin Island, marooned by illness on the Blasket Islands, his kayak stolen in wild Connemara, befriended by Fungi the Dolphin in Dingle.

More than a travelogue, *Dances With Waves* weaves maritime myth and song, seafaring lore and natural history into an absorbing journey around Ireland and the heart of Irish culture and its people.

With beautiful full-colour photographs and maps of the journey.

Paperback £8.99

THE GOLDEN BOOK OF IRELAND

Text: Frances Power/Photographs: Ghigo Roli

Over 200 stunning, original photographs of Ireland, North and South, featuring its historic places, monuments, breathtaking scenery, the people, fairs and festivals. Each photograph is accompanied by fact-filled, informative text on the history, legends, lives and customs covered by the pictures.

Also available in French, German and Italian.

Paperback £7.99

WEST OF IRELAND WALKS

Kevin Corcoran

Explore the counties of Clare, Galway and Mayo in the company of a wildlife expert.

The Walks: The Cliffs of Moher, The Burren: Sliabh

Eilbhe, Blackhead, Abbey Hill, Inishmore, Casla Bog, Errisbeg Mountain (Roundstone), Maumturk Mountains, Kylemore Abbey, Killary Harbour, Cong, Lough Nadirkmore (Partry Mountains), Tonakeera Point, Croagh Patrick.

Paperback £5.99

KERRY WALKS
Kevin Corcoran

This book covers the major scenic areas of Kerry with 20 accessible walks around Kenmare, Killarney, Dingle, Iveragh Peninsula and North Kerry. Illustrated with the author's drawings.

The Walks: Great Blasket Island, Lough Acoose, Bolus Head, Lough Currane, Derrynane, Rossbeigh, Muckross and Knockreer, amongst others.

Paperback £5.99

WEST CORK WALKS
Kevin Corcoran

This helpful guide details ten different walks spread across West Cork, giving clear instructions, with accompanying maps, for each walk, the approximate length of time the walk should take, equipment required and notable features along the way. Casual strollers, family groups, ramblers and serious walkers are all catered for.

The Walks: The Gearagh (near Macroom), Ballyvourney, Gougane Barra, Coolkelure (near Bantry), Castlefreke (near Rosscarbery), Lough Hyne (near Skibbereen), Mizen Head, Priest's Leap (near Glengarriff), Glengarriff and Allihies.

Paperback £5.99

THE COMPLETE WICKLOW WAY
J.B. Malone

The Wicklow Way is a signposted walking trail from Marlay Park in South Dublin over the hills and glens of Wicklow, suitable for the beginner and expert alike.

'The Garden of Ireland', Wicklow is known for its great beauty and variety: heather, woodland, peat bogs, rushing streams, jagged rocks and 'real mountains up to the sky' (J.M.Synge). Famous places with wonderful names: Glencree, Glenmalure, Glendalough, Powerscourt, Lough Dan, Annamoe and Laragh.

Contents include several step-by-step walks, shorter walks and variations, 83 detailed maps, recommended walking gear, bus routes, car parking and safety notes.

Paperback £5.99

IRISH STONE WALLS
Patrick McAfee

This unique guide by expert stonemason Patrick McAfee explores the history of this ancient tradition, giving illustrated examples and step-by-step instructions on constructing, conserving and repairing stone walls of all types, whether dry-stone or mortar.

Contents include: history of stone in Ireland, how to build dry-stone and mortar walls, basic and more advanced techniques, do's and don'ts of repair work.

Hardback £14.99

STONE BUILDINGS
Patrick McAfee

The follow-up book to the best-selling *Irish Stone Walls*. How to build, conserve or renovate stone buildings in the authentic way, using age-old techniques.

The author, a stonemason and conservation consultant, shows how traditional stone buildings were originally constructed; he outlines the traditional techniques, tells how the stone was worked and details the proper methods of repair and maintenance. As well as dealing with stone, the book also covers lime mortars and other traditional finishes. Much of the information is practical, hands-on and intended for the enthusiastic householder as well as the more experienced builder.

Hardback £18.99

Send for our full colour catalogue

ORDER FORM

Please send me the books as marked

I enclose cheque/postal order for £ . . . . (+£1.00 P&P per title)

OR please charge my credit card ☐ Access/Mastercard ☐ Visa

Card Number __ __ __ __   __ __ __ __   __ __ __ __   __ __ __ __

Expiry Date __ __/__ __

Name. . . . . Tel: . . . .

Address . . . .

. . . .

Please send orders to : THE O'BRIEN PRESS, 20 Victoria Road, Dublin 6.

Tel: +353 1 4923333 Fax: + 353 1 4922777 email: books@obrien.ie

Internet:http://www.obrien.ie
